THE
DREAM
THAT WILL
NOT DIE

THE
DREAM
THAT WILL
NOT DIE

*Inspiring Words of John,
Robert, and Edward Kennedy*

Compiled by Brian M. Thomsen
with Douglas Niles

A Tom Doherty Associates Book
New York

My heartfelt thanks go to all those who worked so hard to bring one of Brian's final projects to fruition, especially Bill Fawcett, Douglas Niles, Paul Thomsen, and Frank Weimann.

Brian was a good man who surrounded himself with good people, and he will live on in our hearts.

—DONNA THOMSEN

When he shall die take him and cut him
out into stars and he shall make the face of
heaven so fine that all the world will be in
love with night and pay no worship to the
garish sun.

Bobby Kennedy, quoting from
Shakespeare's *Romeo and Juliet*
Democratic National Convention
Atlantic City, New Jersey, August 27, 1964

THE
DREAM
THAT WILL
NOT DIE

AN AMERICAN
DYNASTY

*The Legacy of Joseph and
Rosemary Kennedy*

What are you going to do with your life?
Kennedys don't just sit around. They do
something.

JOSEPH KENNEDY, QUESTION TO
EACH OF HIS CHILDREN

When three brothers all reach positions of influence and prominence in public life, it is
only natural to consider the combined influence of
heredity and upbringing. In the case of John, Robert,
and Edward Kennedy, these influences can be clearly

traced to a strong and influential parental team. Joseph and Rosemary Kennedy, in separate ways, had a powerful, obvious, and profound impact on their children's lives.

Joseph Patrick Kennedy (1888–1969) was the grandson of an Irish immigrant and the son of a state legislator. Because his father had fought his way out of poverty to a position of some prominence, Joe was able to attend a good prep school (Boston Latin School) and won entrance to Harvard, from which he graduated in 1912.

Meanwhile, Rose Fitzgerald (1890–1995) was the eldest daughter of a prominent Boston politician, John F. "Honey Fitz" Fitzgerald, who served a term in Congress and was twice mayor of Boston. Like her future husband she, too, was a second generation descendent of Irish immigrants who had come to the United States during the years of the potato famine.

After a long, persistent courtship, Joe overcame Honey Fitz's misgivings—Rose's father wasn't entirely certain that the son of a small-time politician was good enough for the daughter of Boston's most prominent Catholic family—and the pair married in 1914. Their first child, Joseph, or Joe Jr., was born in 1915, and by the time Edward, or Teddy, was born in 1932, he was the last of nine children—four sons and five daughters.

A FRUITFUL FAMILY TREE

The Children of Joseph and Rosemary Kennedy

Joseph Jr. (b. 1915)

John (b. 1917)

Rosemary (b. 1918)

Kathleen (b. 1920)

Eunice (b. 1921)

Robert (b. 1925)

Jean (b. 1928)

Edward (b. 1932)

Both parents set strong examples for their children, and both were determined to escape the "second-class citizen" status reserved for Catholics in predominantly Protestant New England.

Joe was particularly driven to succeed in business, becoming a bank president by the time he was twenty-five years old. By thirty, he was a millionaire, involved with shipbuilding, moviemaking, and the Democratic Party. By 1929 he was wealthy enough to establish million-dollar trusts for each of his children and astute enough to avoid losing his shirt in the stock-market crash and subsequent depression. President Franklin Delano Roosevelt appointed him to be the first chairman of the Securities and Exchange Commission in 1934. In 1937 Joe Kennedy became the first Irish American to serve as the United States ambassador to Great Britain.

At home, the Kennedys raised their children to be inquisitive, voracious readers and extremely competitive. The bar for achievement was set very high. Yet both parents also loved their children unconditionally. From Rose, the children learned the importance of compassion and empathy, while Joe made sure that each also was ready to work hard and strive for distinction in public life. Their family home, at Hyannis Port, Massachusetts, would serve as a refuge, a place of calm and serenity, throughout the family members' lives.

From birth, Joe and Rose's eldest son, Joe Jr., was groomed for the role of president of the United States, since both parents shared this vision of their son's destiny. His death while flying a volunteer combat mission during World War II was the first example of what would eventually be called the Kennedy tragedy, and it shifted the burden of expectations to his younger brothers' shoulders.

Joe suffered a stroke in 1961 and was an invalid until he died in 1969. Rose would live to the age of 104, though during the last decade of her life she was confined to a wheelchair. Her generous philanthropy continued late into her life, and at age 90 she led the grandparents' parade in the Special Olympics. She is reputedly the longest-lived presidential relative in US history.

———◆———

"Don't hesitate to interrupt me, whether I am at a meeting, in conference, or visiting with friends, if you wish to consult me about my children."

Joseph Kennedy, instruction to his children's nurse,
Alice Cahill Bastian

•

"A mother knows that hers is the influence which can make that little precious being to be a leader of men, an inspiration, a shining light in the world."

Rose Kennedy

•

"He has called on the best that was in us. There was no such thing as half-trying. Whether it was running a race or catching a football, competing in school—we were to try. And we were to try harder than anyone else."

From the eulogy for Joseph Kennedy, written by
Bobby in 1967, delivered by Teddy in 1969

JOHN FITZGERALD KENNEDY

"Jack"

May 29, 1917–November 22, 1963

And so, my fellow Americans: ask not what your country can do for you—ask what you can do for your country.

INAUGURAL ADDRESS

JANUARY 20, 1961

As the second son of Joe and Rose Kennedy, John, or Jack as he was known, grew up with his sights set on the world of intellectual pursuits, including academics, writing, and publishing, while his older brother carried the family's standard proudly into the world of politics. When Joe Jr. perished in 1944, however, the weight of the Kennedy destiny fell squarely on JFK's shoulders.

Like all of his siblings, Jack grew up in the Kennedy household's competitive, challenging environment. Despite health problems, including chronic back pain and Addison's disease, he thrived in school and graduated from Harvard in 1940. His senior thesis, based on observations he made while serving in London as his father's secretary in the late 1930s, was expanded into his first book: *Why England Slept* became a bestseller during World War II.

In 1941 Jack joined the United States Navy, commanding a patrol-torpedo boat in the crucial Solomon

Islands campaign. When his boat, PT-109, was sunk by collision with a Japanese destroyer, he was badly injured and stranded with his crew far from American positions. Even so, he led all of his surviving crewmen to safety and was awarded a medal for heroism.

In 1946 he began his political career, a career during which he never lost an election. At twenty-nine, he won the congressional seat for Massachusetts's eleventh district. After three terms, during which he established a reputation as a consistent liberal while also being a reliable anti-Communist, he challenged a popular incumbent senator, Henry Cabot Lodge, in 1952. Kennedy won by 70,000 votes, even though the state as a whole voted overwhelmingly for Dwight Eisenhower, the first Republican president in twenty years.

Moving more solidly into liberal territory during his first term in the Senate, Kennedy also married Jacqueline Lee Bouvier (on September 12, 1953) and wrote a book of essays, *Profiles in Courage*, which was awarded a Pulitzer Prize in 1957. When he ran for re-election in 1958, he was already a well-known national figure, and he carried his Senate race by 875,000 votes—still the largest margin in Massachusetts history for a statewide race. Jackie and John had two children, Caroline (b. 1957) and John Jr. (b. 1960, sixteen days after his father was elected president.)

In January 1960, JFK announced his candidacy for the Democratic nomination for the presidency. He quickly dispelled the myth that a Roman Catholic could not win a national election with a strong showing in the primary election in heavily Protestant West Virginia. One Democratic opponent, Hubert Humphrey, withdrew from the race after the dramatic Kennedy win in Wisconsin's primary; his other opponent, Lyndon Johnson, would eventually be named as JFK's vice presidential candidate, unifying the party.

The general election, against Eisenhower's vice president, Richard Nixon, was a close affair, but

Kennedy won by just over 100,000 votes (out of 68,000,000 cast). Despite the closeness of the election, Kennedy would become an extremely popular president. His and Jackie's charisma and charm made an impression around the world, and after a few initial missteps, JFK quickly learned on the job. He successfully challenged Soviet chairman, Nikita Khrushchev, over Berlin and, most dramatically, during the Cuban Missile Crisis of October 1962.

Kennedy's liberal policies were also reflected in the creation of the Peace Corps and the Alliance for Progress (Alianza) in Latin America. In the summer of 1963 Kennedy successfully persuaded Khrushchev and the British prime minister, Harold MacMillan, to join him in signing the nuclear test-ban treaty. Two more of his cherished initiatives, income tax cuts and civil rights legislation, would be passed after his death.

Jack Kennedy was convinced that he could defeat Barry Goldwater, the presumptive Republican nominee for 1964, by a landslide. However, one restive area in the Democratic party lay in the state of Texas. To help mend fences between two rivals in his own party, he scheduled a trip to the state in November 1963. On November 22 JFK was riding through Dallas in an open limousine when he was killed by an assassin who used a sniper rifle.

His death sent the nation into grief. After an unforgettable motorcade through Washington DC, he was laid to rest in Arlington National Cemetery. An eternal flame, first ignited by Jack's widow, remains alight at his grave.

———⊙———

"We shall neither commit nor provoke aggression . . . we shall neither flee nor invoke the threat of force . . . we shall never negotiate out of fear, and we shall never fear to negotiate."

Address to the United Nations General Assembly

September 25, 1961

Timeline—A Cold, Cold War

April, 1948–May, 1949 American and Allied forces supply the city of Berlin by aircraft when the Soviets block train access to the city within East Germany. After thirteen months, the "Berlin Airlift" ends when the Russians abandon the blockade.

June 1950–July 1953 The Korean War is fought between the Communist forces of North Korea and a United Nations coalition army defending the south; the war ends in a cease-fire but not a peace treaty.

May 8, 1954 Vietnamese forces defeat the French army at Dien Bien Phu, leading to the partition of Vietnam with Ho Chi Minh's Communist government taking power in the north.

December 2, 1954 The Senate votes 67 to 22 to condemn Senator Joseph R. McCarthy for conduct unbecoming a Senator, even as McCarthy vows to continue his anti-Communist inquiry, which will now target workers in the defense industry.

February 22, 1955 The United States tests a proto type missile with an atomic warhead in Nevada.

May 14, 1955 The Warsaw Pact is created, unifying the Communist nations of Eastern Europe under the military command of the Soviet Union.

February, 1956 More than one hundred African-Americans in Montgomery, Alabama, are arrested for boycotting the city's buses as they protest segregated seating rules.

October 23, 1956 Hungarians protesting Communist rule are fired on by police, and within days Soviet troops move in, killing some 10,000 while smashing the monthlong rebellion.

October 4, 1957 The Soviet Union announces the launching of Sputnik, the first man-made satellite to successfully orbit the Earth.

August 7, 1958 The nuclear-powered submarine, USS *Nautilus*, concludes a historic two-week voyage underneath the polar ice cap.

January 16, 1959 Fidel Castro's guerrilla army overthrows the Cuban regime of the dictator Fulgencio Batista; the US quickly recognizes the new government, which is not yet Communist.

May 17, 1960 An American U2 spy plane is shot down over the USSR, which results in the cancellation of an upcoming summit meeting between President Eisenhower and the Soviet chairman, Khrushchev, and drives a chilly wedge into East-West relations.

January 3, 1961 The US breaks relations as Castro's increasingly left-leaning government continues to nationalize private businesses, many of them American owned.

April 20, 1961 A CIA-planned invasion on Cuba at the Bay of Pigs, poorly conceived and woefully understrength, ends in disaster; President Kennedy accepts responsibility.

June 4, 1961 An apparently ailing President Kennedy is rudely taken to task by Chairman Khrushchev at the Vienna Summit.

August 13, 1961 The Soviets and East Germans build a wall to divide the city of Berlin, as relations between the superpowers grow increasingly frosty.

September 11, 1962 The Kremlin warns the US that any American attack against Cuba would lead to nuclear war.

October 22, 1962 President Kennedy announces that the US has discovered the presence of Soviet long-range nuclear missiles in Cuba and declares that the US Navy will quarantine Cuba to prevent the delivery of more weapons. For a week the world teeters at the brink of nuclear war, until JFK and Khrushchev reach a deal in which the Soviet missiles are withdrawn.

June 26, 1963 The president speaks at the Berlin wall to hundreds of thousands of Germans, pledging American solidarity with their plight.

August 28, 1963 Declaring "I have a dream," Dr. Martin Luther King Jr. delivers a powerful speech to more than 200,000 peaceful civil rights protestors in Washington DC.

November 24, 1963 Lee Harvey Oswald, JFK's assassin, is shot to death in the Dallas jail.

A Senator Comes of Age

Jack Kennedy spent his time in the Senate formulating the ideas that would guide him and the nation when he was elected president. Even during the 1950s his commitment to humanity and justice was clear.

———◦◦◦———

"Actions and foresight are the only possible preludes to freedom."

August 21, 1957

•

"Every American is now involved in the world. Arms and science alone will not save us. In our concern for the future of America we dare not neglect the education of its politicians. . . . The duty of a scholar—particularly in a republic such as ours—is to contribute his objective views and his sense of liberty to the affairs of his state and nation."

June 16, 1958

·

"Ancient man survived the more powerful beasts about him because his wisdom, his strategies and his policies—overcame his lack of power. We can do the same. We dare not attempt less."

August 14, 1958

·

"Imported democracy is never as meaningful or viable as the domestic brand."

December 15, 1958

•

"Irrational barriers and ancient prejudices fall quickly when the question of survival itself is at stake."

April 12, 1959

•

"Freedom and security are but opposite sides of the same coin—and the free expression of ideas is not more expendable, but far more essential, in a period of challenge and crisis. Without freedom of speech, freedom of assembly, freedom of religion, freedom of the press, equal protection under the laws, and other inalienable rights, men could not govern themselves intelligently.

"The Bill of Rights is the guardian of our security as well as our liberty. Let us not be afraid of debate or dissent—let us encourage it. For if we should ever abandon these basic American traditions in the name of fighting Communism, what would it profit us to win the whole world when we have lost our soul?"

April 16, 1959

•

"To sound the alarm is not to panic but to seek actions from an aroused public. For as the poet Dante once said: 'The hottest places in hell are reserved for those who in a time of great moral crisis seek to preserve their neutrality.'"

September 16, 1959

•

"One cannot stand still. As others change, so must we, if we wish to maintain our relative political or economic condition."

October 13, 1959

•

"There are no magic policies of liberation—there is only hard work—but that hard work can and must be done."

October 17, 1959

•

"No sane society chooses to commit national suicide."

December 11, 1959

A Campaign for a New American Frontier

Jack Kennedy established a tone of change and a theme of progress for his campaign. In one of his first campaign speeches, delivered shortly after Eisenhower's 1960 State of the Union address, he defined his vision of national leadership as contrasting starkly with President Eisenhower's. Note that JFK spoke then, and thereafter, with the assumption that his audience had an understanding and appreciation of American history and ideals.

"Not since the days of Woodrow Wilson has any candidate spoken on the presidency itself before the votes have been irrevocably cast. Let us hope that the 1960 campaign, in addition to discussing the familiar issues where our positions too often blur, will also talk about the presidency itself, as an instrument for dealing with those issues, as an office with varying roles, powers, and limitations. . . .

"During the past eight years, we have seen one concept of the presidency at work. Our needs and hopes have been eloquently stated, but the initiative and follow-through have too often been left to others. . . .

"'The President is at liberty, both in law and conscience, to be as big a man as he can.' So wrote Professor Woodrow Wilson. But President Wilson discovered that to be a big man in the White House inevitably brings cries of dictatorship.

"So did Lincoln and Jackson and the two Roosevelts. And so may the next occupant of that office, if he is the man the times demand. But how much better it would be, in the turbulent sixties, to have a Roosevelt or a Wilson than to have another James Buchanan, cringing in the White House, afraid to move. . . ."

Address to the National Press Club

January 14, 1960

•

37

"I am a Catholic. Does that mean I can't be President of the United States? I'm able to serve in Congress, and my brother was able to give his life, but we can't be President?"

Addressing a crowd

Charleston, South Carolina

On gaining the Democratic nomination for the presidency, JFK defined many of his goals in a powerful acceptance speech and claimed the slogan that would define not just his campaign but his presidency: the new frontier.

"I hope that no American, considering the really critical issues facing this country, will waste his franchise voting either for me or against me solely on account of my religious affiliations. I am telling you now what you are entitled to know: that my decisions on any public policy will be my own—as an American, a Democrat, and a free man. . . ."

In that speech, Kennedy went on to acknowledge the popularity of the current president while getting in a jab at his Republican opponent:

"For just as historians tell us that Richard I was not fit to fill the shoes of bold Henry II—and that Richard Cromwell was not fit to wear the mantle of his uncle—they might add in future years that Richard Nixon did not measure to the footsteps of Dwight D. Eisenhower. . . ."

Not that Eisenhower didn't have his own failings, JFK goes on to suggest:

"Perhaps we could better afford a Coolidge following a Harding, and perhaps we could afford a Pierce following Fillmore. But after Buchanan this nation needed a Lincoln—after Taft we needed a Wilson—after Hoover we needed Franklin Roosevelt. . . .

"And after eight years of drugged and fitful sleep, this nation needs strong, creative, Democratic leadership in the White House. . . .

"I stand here tonight, facing west, upon what was once the last frontier. From the lands that stretched three thousand miles behind us, the pioneers gave up their safety, their comfort, and sometimes their lives, to build our new west. . . .

"Some would say that those struggles are all over, that all the horizons have been explored, that all the battles have been won, that there is no longer an American frontier. But I trust that no one in this assemblage would agree with that sentiment. For the problems are not all solved, and the battles are not all won, and we stand today on the edge of a new frontier. . . ."

Acceptance speech, Democratic Nation Convention

Los Angeles, California

July 15, 1960

*The television debates between JFK and Nixon have
achieved near legendary status in America's political memory. The common misconception, however, that Kennedy
won the debates merely because he "looked better" is belied
by the eloquence of his oratory:*

"In the election of 1960 . . . the question is whether
the world will exist half slave or half free, whether it
will move in the direction of freedom, in the direction
of the road we are taking, or whether it will move in
the direction of slavery. . . .

"Therefore, I think the question before the American people is: Are we doing as much as we can do?
Are we as strong as we should be? Are we as strong as
we must be if we are going to maintain our indepen-
dence, and if we're going to maintain and hold out the
hand of friendship to those who look to us for assistance, to those who look to us for survival?

"I should make it very clear that I do not think

we're doing enough, that I am not satisfied as an American with the progress we are making. . . .

"I saw cases in West Virginia, here in the United States, where children took home part of their school lunch in order to feed their families . . . I'm not satisfied when many of our teachers are inadequately paid . . . I'm not satisfied when I see men like Jimmy Hoffa . . . still free. . . .

"I think we can do better."

First debate

Chicago, Illinois

September 26, 1960

The civil rights issue was regarded as fraught with peril for either candidate. Still, Kennedy made this reply when questioned about it:

"There is a very strong moral basis for this concept of equality before the law. Not only equality before the law but also equality of opportunity. We are in a very difficult time. We need all the talent we can get. . . . We are a goldfish bowl before the world. We have to practice what we preach, and I believe the President of the United States should indicate that."

Second debate

Washington DC

October 7, 1960

An Inaugural Address for the Ages

There were only a few inaugural addresses in the twentieth century that really left a profound impact on the American psyche. Before 1960, the most memorable was certainly Franklin Delano Roosevelt's admonition at the beginning of his first term in 1933 that "the only thing we have to fear is fear itself."

As he took office in January, 1961, Kennedy wanted to

deliver an equally powerful and memorable address. With the aid of his chief speechwriter, Ted Sorensen—and with both of them using Lincoln's Gettysburg Address as an example and an ideal—he crafted one of the most powerful speeches in American history, stirringly delivering it from the steps of the nation's Capitol building on January 20, 1961. At less than 1,500 words, it was only half as long as the typical inaugural speech, but many of the concepts and phrases still live on.

"We observe today not a victory of party, but a celebration of freedom—symbolizing an end, as well as a beginning—symbolizing renewal, as well as change. . . .

"The world is very different now. For man holds in his mortal hands the power to abolish all forms of human poverty and all forms of human life. And yet the same revolutionary beliefs for which our forebears fought are still at issue around the globe—the belief that the rights of man come not from the generosity of the state, but from the hand of God. . . .

"Let the word go forth from this time and place, to friend and foe alike, that the torch has been passed to a new generation of Americans—born in this century, tempered by war, disciplined by a hard and bitter peace, proud of our ancient heritage, and unwilling to witness or permit the slow undoing of those human rights to which this nation has always been committed, and to which we are committed today at home and around the world.

"Let every nation know, whether it wishes us well or ill, that we shall pay any price, bear any burden, meet any hardship, support any friend, oppose any foe, to assure the survival and success of liberty.

"This much we pledge—and more.

"To those old allies whose cultural and spiritual origins we share, we pledge the loyalty of faithful friends. . . .

"To those new States whom we welcome to the ranks of the free, we pledge our word that one form of colonial control shall not have passed away merely to be replaced by a far more iron tyranny. . . .

"To those peoples in the huts and villages of half the globe struggling to break the bonds of mass misery, we pledge our best efforts to help them help themselves, for whatever period is required—not because the Communists may be doing it, not because we seek their votes, but because it is right. If a free society cannot save the many who are poor, it cannot help the few who are rich. . . .

"Finally, to those nations who would make themselves our adversary, we offer not a pledge but a request: that both sides begin anew the quest for peace, before the dark powers of destruction unleashed by science engulf all humanity in planned or accidental self-destruction.

"We dare not tempt them with weakness. For only when our arms are sufficient beyond doubt can we be certain beyond doubt that they will never be employed. . . .

"So let us begin anew, remembering on both sides that civility is not a sign of weakness, and sincerity is always subject to proof. Let us never negotiate out of fear, but let us never fear to negotiate.

"Let both sides explore what problems unite us instead of belaboring those problems which divide us. . . . Let both sides seek to invoke the wonders of science instead of its terrors. Together let us explore the stars, conquer the deserts, eradicate disease, tap the ocean depths, and encourage the arts and commerce. Let both sides unite to heed in all corners of the earth the command of Isaiah—to 'undo the heavy burdens [and] let the oppressed go free.'

"And if a beachhead of cooperation can push back the jungle of suspicion, let both sides join in creating a new endeavor, not a balance of power but a new world of law, where the strong are just and the weak secure and the peace preserved. . . .

"In the long history of the world, only a few generations have been granted the role of defending freedom in its hour of maximum danger. I do not shrink from this responsibility—I welcome it! I do not believe that any of us would exchange places with any other people, or any other generation. The energy, the faith, the devotion which we bring to this endeavor will light our country and all who serve it—and the glow from that fire can truly light the world.

"And so, my fellow Americans: ask not what your country can do for you—ask what you can do for your country. . . ."

The Cold Warrior

"Compromise need not mean cowardice. Indeed, it is frequently the compromisers and conciliators who are faced with the severest tests of political courage."

Profiles in Courage

.

"Mankind must do away with war, or war will do away with mankind."

Speech to the United Nations General Assembly

September 25, 1961

.

"Then, Mr. Chairman, there will be war. It will be a cold winter."

To Nikita Khrushchev, when Khrushchev refused to compromise on the issue of Berlin

Vienna summit

June 4, 1961

The crisis over Berlin in the summer of 1961 brought the two superpowers to the brink of war, as JFK refused to give in to Khrushchev's demand that the NATO powers abandon the city to Communist control. Speaking to the nation by television, President Kennedy gave one of the most frightening speeches in American history.

"We are clear about what must be done, and we intend to do it. I want to talk frankly to you tonight about the first steps we shall take. These actions will require sacrifice on the part of many of our citizens. More will be required in the future. They will require, from all of us, courage and perseverance in the years to come. But if we and our allies act out of strength and unity of purpose—with calm determination and steady nerves—using restraint in our words as well as our weapons, I am hopeful that both peace and freedom will be sustained. . . .

"We do not want to fight, but we have fought

before. . . . Those who threaten to unleash the forces of war on a dispute over West Berlin should recall the words of the ancient philosopher: 'A man who causes fear cannot be free from fear.' . . . We cannot negotiate with those who say 'what's mine is mine, and what's yours in negotiable.'

"In the coming months I hope to let every citizen know what steps he can take to protect his family in case of attack. . . . In the event of an attack, the lives of those families which are not hit in a nuclear blast and fire can still be saved—if they can be warned to take shelter and if that shelter is available. . . .

"When I ran for the Presidency of the United States, I knew that this country faced serious challenges, but I could not realize—nor could any man realize, who does not bear the burden of this office—how heavy and constant would be those burdens.

"Three times in my lifetime our country and Europe have been involved in major wars. In each case serious misjudgments were made on both sides of the intentions of others, which brought about great devastation.

"Now, in the thermonuclear age, any misjudgment on either side about the intentions of the other could rain more devastation in several hours than has been wrought in all the wars of human history. . . ."

Address on the Berlin crisis

July 25, 1961

The tension of the Berlin crisis eased slightly in August 1961, when the construction of the Berlin wall blocked the flow of talented refugees who had been fleeing from east to west.

"Today, every inhabitant of this planet must contemplate the day when this planet may no longer be inhabitable. Every man, woman, and child lives under a nuclear sword of Damocles, hanging by the slenderest of threads, capable of being cut at any moment by accident or miscalculation or madness. The weapons of war must be abolished before they demolish us."

Address to the United Nations General Assembly

September 25, 1961

The Cold War reached its most frightening moment during the Cuban Missile Crisis. A week after learning of the buildup of Soviet nuclear weapons on that island nation, JFK addressed the nation in a stunning televised address.

"This government, as promised, has maintained the closest surveillance of the Soviet military buildup upon the island of Cuba. Within the past week, unmistakable evidence has established the fact that a series of offensive missile sites is now in preparation on that imprisoned island. The purpose of these bases can be none other than to provide a nuclear strike capability against the Western Hemisphere. . . .

"Each of these missiles, in short, is capable of striking Washington DC, the Panama Canal, Cape Canaveral, Mexico City, or any other city in the southeastern part of the United States, in Central America, or in the Caribbean area. [Other missiles soon to be deployed] could strike targets as far north as Hudson Bay, and as far south as Lima, Peru. . . .

"This nation is opposed to war. We are also true to our word. Our unswerving objective, therefore, must be to prevent the use of these missiles against this or any other country, and to secure their withdrawal from the Western Hemisphere. . . .

"[To the citizens of Cuba] I speak to you as a friend, as one who knows of your deep attachment to your fatherland, as one who shares your aspirations for liberty and justice for all. . . . These new weapons are not in your interest. They contribute nothing for your peace and well-being. They can only undermine it. But this country has no wish to cause you to suffer or to impose any system upon you. We know that your lives and land are being used as pawns by those who deny your freedom. . . .

"Our goal is not the victory of might, but the vindication of right—not peace at the expense of freedom, but both peace and freedom, here in this hemisphere and, we hope, around the world."

October 22, 1962

The president's solution was a quarantine of the waters around Cuba, to be enforced by the US Navy, preventing any Eastern Bloc ship from carrying offensive weapons to the island. Many of his military advisers, most notably Air Force Chief of Staff General Curtis LeMay, ridiculed the measure as "weak" and "appeasement"; they advocated air strikes against the missile sites and an invasion of the island.

"[General LeMay and other commanders] have one great advantage in giving advice. If we listen to them, and do what they want us to do, none of us will be alive later to tell them that they were wrong."

To his brother Bobby,

October 20, 1962

•

"The mere absence of war is not peace. . . . A moment of pause is not a promise of peace."

January 14, 1963

•

"Suspicions on one side breeds suspicion on the other, and new weapons beget counter-weapons."

Commencement speech

American University

June 10, 1963

•

"There are some who say, in Europe and elsewhere, 'We can work the Communists.' Let them come to Berlin. And there are even a few who say that it's true that communism is an evil system but it permits us to make economic progress. . . . Let them come to Berlin. . . .

"All free men, wherever they may live, are citizens of Berlin. . . . *Ich bin ein Berliner!* ["I am a Berliner!"]."

Speech at the Berlin wall

June 26, 1963

·

"Even little wars are dangerous in this nuclear world."

November 8, 1963

·

"A boxer cannot work himself into the proper psychological and physical condition for a fight that he seriously believes will never come off."

Why England Slept

———◦◉◦———

President Kennedy's crowning accomplishment on the subject of nuclear war was the historic agreement signed in July 1963 by Chairman Khrushchev, the British prime minister MacMillan, and JFK himself, which placed stringent limits on the testing of nuclear weapons—each instance of which spread poisonous radiation through the atmosphere. It was one of the rare occasions when he could give a national address on the Cold War that did not address a specific and current crisis.

"I speak to you tonight in a spirit of hope. . . . In an age when both sides have come to possess enough nuclear power to destroy the human race several times over, the world of communism and the world of free choice have been caught up in a vicious circle of conflicting ideology and interest. Each increase in tension has produced an increase of arms;

each increase of arms has produced an increase in tension.

"Yesterday, a shaft of light cut into the darkness. Negotiations were concluded in Moscow on a treaty to ban all nuclear tests in the atmosphere, in outer space, and under water. . . .

"A war today or tomorrow, if it led to nuclear war, would not be like any war in history. A full-scale nuclear exchange, lasting less than sixty minutes, with the weapons now in existence, could wipe out more than three hundred million Americans, Europeans, and Russians, as well as untold numbers elsewhere. And the survivors, as Chairman Khrushchev warned the Communist Chinese, 'the survivors would envy the dead.' For they would inherit a world so devastated by explosions and poison and fire that today we cannot even conceive of its horrors.

"So let us try to turn the world away from war. Let us make the most of this opportunity, and every opportunity, to reduce tension, to slow down the perilous nuclear arms race, and to check the world's slide toward final annihilation. . . ."

National television address

July 26, 1963

Rights and Freedom

"What does justice require? In the end it requires liberty."

Speech at the Berlin wall

June 26, 1963

———

The civil rights movement found a new battleground at the University of Mississippi, in Oxford, when federal agents and Mississippi national guardsmen escorted an African-

American student, James Meredith, onto the campus. The Mississippi troops abruptly withdrew, leaving some five hundred marshals surrounded and vastly outnumbered by angry mobs of segregationists. President Kennedy made a 10 p.m. television address to try and calm the situation.

"Mister James Meredith is now in residence on the campus of the University of Mississippi. This has been accomplished thus far without the use of National Guard or other troops. And it is to be hoped that the law enforcement officers of the state of Mississippi and the federal marshals will continue to be sufficient for the future. . . .

"Mississippi and her University are noted for their courage, for the contribution of talent and thought to the affairs of this nation. . . . You have a great tradition to uphold, a tradition of honor and courage won on the field of battle and on the gridiron as well as the university campus. . . . The eyes of the nation and all of the world are upon you and upon all of us, and the honor of your university and state are in the balance."

September 30, 1962

———◦◉◦———

Unfortunately, the remarks were already overtaken by events, as some of the mob began shooting at the federal marshals, who suffered more than a hundred injured in the Battle of Ole Miss. A reporter and an innocent bystander were killed before the army moved in at 4 a.m. to impose order.

"People are dying in Oxford! This is the worst thing I've seen in forty-five years."

While waiting for the army units to arrive

October 1, 1962

•

"Can those damn things reach Oxford, Mississippi?"

Asked of a CIA briefer regarding Soviet missiles in Cuba

October 16, 1962

•

"Thomas Jefferson once said that if you expect a people to be ignorant and free you expect what never was and never will be."

February 16, 1962

•

"We must all, in our daily lives, live up to the age-old faith that peace and freedom walk together. In too many of our cities today, the peace is not secure, because the freedom is incomplete."

Commencement speech

American University

June 10, 1963

———◦———

The increasingly violent civil rights struggle in the United States had been waxing in strength since even before the Montgomery (Alabama) bus boycott in 1956. By the early 1960s, it threatened to explode into full-blown conflict. After Governor George Wallace of Alabama stood at a podium to bar the entry of two black students into the University of Alabama on June 11, 1963, President Kennedy immediately went on the air to deliver a landmark speech on civil rights in America.

"The Negro baby born in America today, regardless of the section of the nation in which he is born, has about one-half as much chance of completing . . . high school as a white baby born in the same place on the same day, one-third as much chance of completing college, one-third as much chance of becoming a professional man, twice as much chance of becoming unemployed, about one-seventh as much chance of earning $10,000 a year, a life expectancy which is seven years shorter, and the prospects of earning only half as much.

"This is not a sectional issue . . . nor is it a partisan issue. . . . This is not even a legal or legislative issue alone. It is better to settle these matters in the courts than on the streets, and new laws are needed at every level, but law alone cannot make men see right.

"We are confronted primarily with a moral issue. It is as old as the scriptures and is as clear as the American constitution. . . .

"If an American, because his skin is dark, cannot eat lunch in a restaurant open to the public, if he cannot send his children to the best public school available . . . if he cannot enjoy the full and free lives which all of us want, then who among us would be . . . content to live with the counsels of patience and delay?

"Today we are committed to a worldwide struggle

to promote and protect the rights of all who wish to be free. And when Americans are sent to Vietnam or West Berlin, we do not ask for whites only. . . .

"It ought to be possible . . . for every American to enjoy the privileges of being American without regard to his race or color. . . . In short, every American ought to have the right to be treated as he would wish to be treated, as one would wish his children to be treated. . . .

"The problem must be solved in the homes of every American in every community across our country. . . ."

Report on civil rights

June 11, 1963

•

"Every American has the right to a decent life for himself and a better life for his children."

November 18, 1963

———◆———

Jack Kennedy's last book, A Nation of Immigrants, *was written in 1958 at the request of the Anti-Defamation League. Originally drafted as an extensive essay, it was published posthumously as a complete book.*

"The contributions of immigrants can be seen in every aspect of national life. We see it in religion, in politics, in business, in the arts, in education, even in athletics and in entertainment. There is no part of our nation that has not been touched by our immigrant background. . . .

"Every ethnic minority, in seeking its own freedom, helped strengthen the fabric of liberty in American life. Similarly, every aspect of the American economy has profited from the contributions of immigrants. . . .

"Immigration policy should be generous; it should

be fair; it should be flexible. With such a policy we can turn to the world, and to our own past, with clean hands and a clear conscience. . . .

"We have come to realize in modern times that the 'melting pot' need not mean the end of particular ethnic identities or traditions."

A Nation of Immigrants

An Ambitious Agenda

While some liberals felt that Kennedy, hampered as he was by the Cold War, didn't do enough to advance their causes, he in fact initiated some far-reaching programs in the areas of human rights and technology. The legacies of these ideas remain in place today.

The first, accomplished six weeks into his presidency, was the creation of the Peace Corps. It was an idea he had broached in his campaign.

"How many of you who are going to be doctors are willing to spend your days in Ghana? Technicians or engineers, how many of you are willing to work in the Foreign Service and spend your lives traveling around the world?"

Speech at the University of Michigan

October 14, 1960

•

"I propose a peace corps of talented young men and women, willing and able to serve their country . . . for three years as an alternative or as a supplement to peacetime selective service."

Speech in San Francisco

November 2, 1960

•

"I have today signed an executive order providing for the establishment of a peace corps. . . . This corps will be a pool of trained men and women, sent overseas by the United States government, or through private institutions and organizations, to help foreign countries meet their urgent needs for skilled manpower. It is our hope to have between five hundred and one thousand people in the field by the end of this year. . . .

"It will not be easy. None of the men and women will be paid a salary. They will live at the same level as the citizens of the country which they are sent to, doing the same work, eating the same food, speaking the same language.

"I'm hoping it will be a source of satisfaction to Americans and a contribution to world peace."

Announcement of the creation of the Peace Corps

Washington DC

March 1, 1961

Less than two weeks after putting the Peace Corps into mo-tion, President Kennedy addressed a group of diplomats from Latin America, proposing the Alliance for Progress to pledge American support to the nation's neighbors in the hemisphere.

"As a citizen of the United States, let me be the first to admit that we North Americans have not always grasped the significances of [our] common mission, just as it is true that many in your own countries have not fully understood the urgency of the need to lift people from poverty and ignorance and despair. But we must turn from these mistakes—from the failures and the misunderstandings of the past to a future full of peril, but bright with hope. . . .

"Our Alliance for Progress is an alliance of free governments, and it must work to eliminate tyranny from a hemisphere in which it has no rightful place. Therefore, let us express our special friendship to the people of

Cuba and the Dominican Republic—and the hope that they will soon rejoin the society of free men, uniting with us in a common effort. . . .

"Our nations are the products of a common struggle, the revolt from colonial rule. And our people share a common heritage—the quest for dignity and the freedom of man. . . .

"And so I say to the men and women of the Americas—to the *campesino* in the fields, to the *obrero* in the cities, to the *estudiente* in the schools—prepare your mind and heart for the task ahead . . . so that your children and our children in this hemisphere can find an ever richer and a freer life."

Proposal of the Alliance for Progress

Washington DC

March 13, 1961

•

"How was my Spanish?"

> To the speechwriter Richard Goodwin,
>
> following the above speech

"Perfect," Goodwin politely, if not entirely truthfully, replied.

.

"I believe that this nation should commit itself to achieving the goal, before this decade is out, of landing a man on the moon and returning him safely to the earth. No single space project in this period will be more impressive to mankind, or more important for the long-range exploration of space; and none will be so difficult or expensive to accomplish."

> Special message to Congress on urgent national needs
>
> May 25, 1961

.

"But why, some say, the moon? Why choose this as our goal? And they may well ask why climb the highest mountain? Why, thirty-five years ago, fly the Atlantic? . . . Why does Rice play Texas? . . .

"We choose to go to the moon in this decade not because [it is] easy but because [it is] hard, because that goal will serve to organize and measure the best of our energies and skills, because that challenge is one that we are willing to accept, one that we are unwilling to postpone, and one which we intend to win."

Address on space travel

Rice University

September 12, 1962

Inspirational Remarks

"We must always consider that we shall be as a city upon a hill. . . . The eyes of all people are upon us."

Quoting the Puritan leader John Winthrop

Address to the General Court of the

Commonwealth of Massachusetts

January 9, 1961

•

"The hour of decision has arrived. We cannot afford to wait and see what happens while the tide of events sweeps over and beyond us. We must use time as a tool, not as a couch."

December 6, 1961

•

"In whatever arena of life one may meet the challenge of courage . . . [e]ach man must decide for himself the course he will follow. The stories of past courage can define that ingredient—they can teach, they can offer hope, they can provide inspiration. But they cannot supply courage itself. For this each man must look into his own soul."

Profiles in Courage

•

"Let us resolve to be the masters, not the victims, of our history, controlling our own destiny without giving way to blind suspicion and emotion."

October 19, 1963

•

"It is our task, in our times and our generations, to hand down undiminished to those who come after us, as was handed down to us by those who went before, the natural wealth and beauty which is ours."

March 3, 1961

•

"The effort to improve the conditions of man, however, is not a task for the few. It is the task of all nations—acting alone, acting in groups, acting in the United Nations, for plague and pestilence, and plunder and pollution, the hazards of nature, and the hunger of children are the foes of every nation. The earth, the sea, and the air are the concern of every nation. And science, technology, and education can be the ally of every nation.

"Never before has man had such capacity to control his own environment, to end thirst and hunger, to conquer poverty and disease, to banish illiteracy and massive human misery. We have the power to make this the best generation of mankind in the history of the world—or to make it the last."

Address to the United Nations General Assembly

September 20, 1963

•

"In its light we must think and act not only for the moment but for our time. I am reminded of the story of the great French Marshal Lyautey, who once asked his gardener to plant a tree. The gardener objected that the tree was slow-growing and would not reach maturity for a hundred years. The Marshal replied, 'In that case, there is no time to lose, plant it this afternoon.'

"Today a world of knowledge—a world of co-operation—a just and lasting peace—may be years away. But we have no time to lose. Let us plant our trees this afternoon."

Speech at University of California, Berkeley

March 23, 1962

•

"The American by nature is optimistic. He is experimental, an inventor and a builder who builds best when called upon to build greatly. Arouse his will to believe in himself, give him a great goal to believe in, and he will create the means to reach it."

January 1, 1960

•

"Books and libraries and the will to use them are among the most important tools our nation has to diffuse knowledge and to develop our powers of creative wisdom."

April 16, 1961

•

"We need to strengthen our nation by investing in our youth. The future of any country which is dependent upon the will and wisdom of its citizens is damaged, and irreparably damaged, whenever any of its children are not educated to the full extent of their talents, from grade school through graduate school."

January 14, 1963

•

"I am not fearful of the future. We must be patient. We must be courageous. We must accept both risks and burdens, but with the will and the work freedom will prevail."

June 6, 1961

•

"We love our country, not for what it was, though it has always been great—not for what it is, though of this we are deeply proud—but for what it someday can and, through the efforts of us all, someday will be."

February 13, 1961

.

"The problems of the world cannot possibly be solved by skeptics or cynics whose horizons are limited by the obvious realities. We need men who can dream of things that never were. . . ."

Address to the Irish parliament

Dublin, Ireland

June 28, 1963

.

"Does every American boy and girl have an opportunity to develop whatever talents he or she has? All of us do not have equal talent, but all of us should have an equal opportunity to develop our talents."

June 6, 1963

•

"We do not want in the United States a nation of spectators. We want a nation of participants in the vigorous life."

February 21, 1961

•

"Our problems are manmade—therefore, they can be solved by man. And man can be as big as he wants. No problem of human destiny is beyond human beings. Man's reason and spirit have often solved the seemingly unsolvable—and we believe they can do it again."

Commencement speech

American University

June 10, 1963

·

"We have made a beginning—but we have only begun. Now the time has come to make the most of our gains—to translate the renewal of our national strength into the achievement of our national purpose."

State of the Union address

January 11, 1962

Kennedy's Wit

"Forgive your enemies—but never forget their names."

Attributed

———◆———

During his presidential campaign, Jack traveled north and worked hard to win votes in Alaska, where he lost, but neg-

lected to visit Hawaii, where he won, prompting the following remark:

"Just think what my margin would have been if I had never left home at all."

•

"Do you realize the responsibility I carry? I'm the only person standing between Richard Nixon and the White House."

Attributed, during the 1960 presidential campaign

•

"I don't think the intelligence reports are all that hot. Some days I get more out of the *New York Times*."

Attributed

•

"I got where I am by not trusting the experts. But this time I put all my faith in the experts, and look what happened."

To Ted Sorenson, following the Bay of Pigs disaster

•

"I believe in an America where religious intolerance will someday end—where every man has the same right to attend or not attend the church of his choice."

Address to the Ministerial Association of Greater Houston
September 12, 1960

•

"My brother Bob doesn't want to be in government— he promised Dad he'd go straight."

Attributed

•

"I hope you get to keep them."

> Remark to Nikita Khrushchev, about the
> two "peace medals" worn by the Soviet leader
> Vienna summit
> June 3, 1961

•

"The day before my inauguration, President Eisenhower told me, 'you'll find that no easy problems ever come to the President of the United States. If they are easy to solve, someone else has solved them.'"

> Attributed

•

"I always have difficulty recognizing my positions when they are stated by the vice president."

> Third debate
> New York City, New York
> October 13, 1960

•

"[I graduated] from Harvard, which is known as the 'Michigan of the East.'"

Speech at the University of Michigan

October 14, 1960

•

"I think this is the most extraordinary collection of talent, of human knowledge, that has ever been gathered at the White House, with the possible exception of when Thomas Jefferson dined alone."

At a dinner honoring Nobel Prize winners

The White House

April 29, 1962

•

"Mothers all want their sons to grow up to be president, but they don't want them to be politicians in the process."

Attributed

•

"One of the inspiring notes that was struck in the last debate was struck by the vice president in his very moving warning to the children of the nation and the candidates against the use of profanity by Presidents and ex-Presidents when they are on the stump. . . . But I am told that a prominent Republican said to [Vice President Nixon] yesterday in Jacksonville, Florida, 'Mr. Vice President, that was a damn fine speech.' And the vice president said, 'I appreciate the compliment but not the language.' And the Republican went on, 'Yes, sir, I liked it so much that I contributed one thousand dollars to your campaign.' And Mr. Nixon replied 'The hell you say!'"

At the Al Smith Dinner,

with both candidates in attendance

New York, New York

October 16, 1960

•

"A police state finds that it cannot command the grain to grow."

Attributed

———◦◉◦———

Asked by a young boy how he got to be a war hero, JFK replied,

"It was absolutely involuntary. They sank my boat."

•

"There seems to be some disagreement as to whether my grandfather Fitzgerald came from Wexford, Limerick, or Tipperary. And it is even more confusing as to where my great-grandmother came from, because her son—who was the mayor of Boston—used to claim his mother came from whichever Irish county had the most votes in the audience he was addressing at that particular time."

Attributed

When President Kennedy and Jackie traveled to Europe in the summer of 1961, they were treated like royalty in the capitals of America's NATO allies. The French, in particular, were effusive in their welcome of the First Lady, who was a fluent speaker of the language.

"I do not think it entirely inappropriate to introduce myself to this audience. I am the man who accompanied Jacqueline Kennedy to Paris."

Thanking his hosts, including President De Gaulle, after the visit

•

"Mr. Nixon in the last seven days has called me an economic ignoramus, a Pied Piper, and all the rest. I've just confined myself to calling him a Republican, but he says that is getting low."

Remark just before the 1960 election

Eulogy

At the Democratic National Convention in Atlantic City, New Jersey, on August 27, 1964, Senator Robert Kennedy

eulogized his brother in a moving, personal speech that stands as a magnificent example of the Kennedy eloquence and a powerful remembrance of what the nation lost in November 1963.

"... No matter what talent an individual possesses, what energy he might have, no matter how much integrity and how much honesty he might have, if he is by himself, and particularly a political figure, he can accomplish very little. But if he is sustained, as President Kennedy was, by the Democratic Party all over the United States, dedicated to the same things that he was attempting to accomplish, he can accomplish a great deal.

"No one knew that more than President John F. Kennedy. He used to take great pride in telling of the trip that Thomas Jefferson and James Madison made up the Hudson River in 1800 on a botanical expedition searching for butterflies; that they ended up down in

New York City and that they formed the Democratic Party.

"He took great pride in the fact that the Democratic Party was the oldest political party in the world, and he knew that this linkage of Madison and Jefferson with the leaders in New York combined the North and South, and combined the industrial areas of the country with the rural farms and that this combination was always dedicated to progress and all of our Presidents have been dedicated to progress.

"He thought of Thomas Jefferson in the Louisiana Purchase, and also when Jefferson realized that the United States could not remain on the Eastern Seaboard and sent Lewis and Clark to the West Coast; of Andrew Jackson, of Woodrow Wilson; of Franklin Roosevelt who saved our citizens who were in great despair because of the financial crisis; of Harry Truman who not only spoke but acted for freedom.

"So, when he became President he not only had

his own principles and his own ideals but he had the strength of the Democratic Party. As President he wanted to do something for the mentally ill and the mentally retarded; for those who were not covered by Social Security; for those who were not receiving an adequate minimum wage; for those who did not have adequate housing; for our elderly people who had difficulty paying their medical bills; for our fellow citizens who are not white and who had difficulty living in this society. To all this he dedicated himself. . . .

"And that's why he made such an effort and was committed to the young people not only of the United States but to the young people of the world. And in all of these efforts you were there, all of you.

"When there were difficulties, you sustained him. When there were periods of crisis, you stood beside him. When there were periods of happiness, you laughed with him. And when there were periods of sorrow, you comforted him. I realize that as individuals we can't just look back, that we must look forward. . . .

"I realize that as individuals, and even more important, as a political party and as a country, we can't just look to the past, we must look to the future.

"So I join with you in realizing that what started four years ago—what everyone here started four years ago—that is to be sustained; that is to be continued. . . .

"We must [remember] that President Kennedy once said:

"'We have the capacity to make this the best generation in the history of mankind, or make it the last.'

"If we do our duty, if we meet our responsibilities and our obligations, not just as Democrats, but as American citizens in our local cities and towns and farms and our states and in the country as a whole, then this generation of Americans is going to be the best generation in the history of mankind.

"He often quoted from Robert Frost—and said it applied to himself—but we could apply it to the Democratic Party and to all of us as individuals:

'The woods are lovely, dark and deep, but I have promises to keep and miles to go before I sleep, and miles to go before I sleep.'"

ROBERT FRANCIS KENNEDY

"Bobby"

November 20, 1925–June 6, 1968

Some men see things as they are and say,
"Why?" I dream of things that never were
and say, "Why not?"

FIRST CAMPAIGN SPEECH
UNIVERSITY OF KANSAS
MARCH 18, 1968

O f the three Kennedy brothers who rose to political greatness in America, the flame of Bobby's political career burned the most briefly. Nevertheless, in some ways, it might also have been the most intense.

Bobby was the seventh of what would eventually be Joe and Rosemary Kennedy's nine children. A student at Harvard when World War II swept into America in December 1941, Bobby left college to enlist in the navy. After the war, he graduated from Harvard in 1948 and went on to receive a degree from the University of Virginia Law School in 1951. His political life began immediately thereafter, as he returned to Massachusetts to manage Jack's campaign for the United States Senate in 1952.

It is surprising that his first nationally recognized role came in 1953, when he served as assistant counsel on Senator Joseph McCarthy's Permanent Subcommittee on Investigations. He resigned soon thereafter and returned the next year to serve as counsel to the

Democratic minority. In 1957, Bobby began to serve as the counsel to the Senate select subcommittee investigating organized crime, a role that would forever earn him the enmity of the Mafia and other racketeering organizations.

In 1960 Bobby left his role on the subcommittee to manage Jack's presidential campaign. Following his brother's victory, in 1961 Bobby was appointed to JFK's cabinet in the important role of attorney general. Despite his relative youth, he performed aggressively and effectively in the role. He continued his campaign against organized crime with unprecedented vigor, eventually assembling the evidence and witnesses to make the case that would convict Jimmy Hoffa.

He also began to establish his reputation as a strong crusader for civil rights. When he learned on May 20, 1961, that a hostile and armed mob was gathering to directly threaten Martin Luther King Jr. and more than a thousand of his supporters in Montgomery, Alabama, Bobby dispatched four hundred federal agents to protect the civil rights activists. As the racial conflicts in the southern states grew to even more dangerous levels during the early part of the decade, he frequently engaged in long-distance telephone negotiations in an earnest effort to keep the peace and to guarantee the rights of protesters.

When his brother was assassinated on November 22, 1963, Bobby remained as the attorney general in Lyndon Johnson's administration until September 1964, serving in that role for forty-four months. His experiences as the chief law-enforcement officer in the federal government had a profound impact on his beliefs, values, and maturation.

In November of 1964 he was elected with a comfortable margin of victory to the vacant United States Senate seat from New York. Over the next few years he rose to great prominence as an eloquent spokesman for the liberal wing of the Democratic Party and as a sharp critic of President Johnson's conduct of the war in Vietnam. Finally, on March 16, 1968, he announced his candidacy for the Democratic nomination for the presidency in the fall election. He was a popular and eloquent campaigner who captured the enthusiasm of much of the younger generation of voters, as well as those who were adamantly opposed to the increasingly unpopular war.

His campaign, which would last just less than three months, was marked by fervent support, especially from young voters, and a mood of hope and promise. There was a belief in many sectors of the population that a real political sea change was occurring in the country and that it was centered in the liberal wing of the Democratic Party.

By June 4 Bobby had been victorious in five out of six presidential primary elections, including the one held that day in California. It was early in the morning of June 5, shortly after he had addressed a crowd of supporters in the ballroom of the Ambassador Hotel in Los Angeles, when he was gunned down by an assassin. He would be laid to rest in Arlington National Cemetery, very near the grave of his brother, John.

———

"Few will have the greatness to bend history; but each of us can work to change a small portion of the events, and in the total of all these acts will be written the history of this generation. . . . It is from numberless diverse acts of courage and belief that human history is thus shaped. Each time a man stands up for an ideal, or acts to improve the lot of others, or strikes out against injustice, he sends forth a tiny ripple of hope, and crossing each other from a million different centers of energy and daring those ripples build a current which can sweep down the mightiest walls of oppression and resistance."

Day of Affirmation Address

University of Capetown

June 6, 1966

Timeline — A Descent into Chaos

November 29, 1963 President Johnson appoints Chief Justice Earl Warren to head a special commission investigating the assassination of President John F. Kennedy.

February 12, 1964 The Beatles perform their first American concert, on the *Ed Sullivan Show*.

March 12, 1964 Jimmy Hoffa, president of the International Brotherhood of Teamsters, is sentenced to prison on charges of jury tampering.

June 25, 1964 Three civil rights activists are reported missing in Mississippi, after their burned and demolished car is discovered in a rural area.

July 2, 1964 President Johnson signs the Civil Rights Act, the most sweeping rights bill in American history.

August 2–4, 1964 North Vietnamese gunboats reportedly attack US Navy ships in the Gulf of Tonkin, and on August 7 the Gulf of Tonkin Resolution is passed by the House and Senate, awarding President Johnson sweeping authority to deploy the US military against North Vietnam.

November 3, 1964 President Johnson defeats the Republican challenger Barry Goldwater in a landslide of historic proportions; Bobby Kennedy is elected to the Senate.

February 1, 1965 Dr. Martin Luther King Jr. and 770 protesters are arrested in Selma, Alabama, as Sheriff James Clark orders brutal force used in breaking up the civil rights demonstration.

March–April 1965 The United States Air Force and Marines begin to conduct increasingly aggressive actions against Communist insurgents in South Vietnam.

July 28, 1965 President Johnson sends 50,000 more American troops to South Vietnam; two days later he signs a bill creating the Medicare program as part of his "great society" reforms.

August 15, 1965 Race riots erupt in Watts, Los Angeles, resulting in some thirty deaths and a deployment of 20,000 California national guardsmen.

December 25, 1965 A Christmas truce is observed in South Vietnam, where some 154,000 US troops are now deployed; US military deaths in the country since 1961 now total 1,636.

July, 1966 Race riots rage in Chicago, Brooklyn, and Cleveland.

January 6, 1967 United States and South Vietnamese troops commence a massive attack on the Vietcong stronghold known as the Iron Triangle.

July 30, 1967 General William Westmoreland requests more US troops in South Vietnam, declaring, "We are winning slowly but steadily."

October 21, 1967 At least 50,000 demonstrators march from the Lincoln Memorial to the Pentagon, where they scuffle violently with soldiers and federal marshals.

January 31, 1968 Belying American claims of progress in the war, Vietnamese communists launch the Tet offensive, a massive series of attacks that, while militarily unsuccessful, underscore the enemy's commitment to carry on the fight.

March 31, 1968 Wearied by the unsuccessful pursuit of the Vietnam War, President Johnson stuns the nation by announcing that he will not seek re-election.

April 4, 1968 Dr. Martin Luther King Jr. is assassinated in Memphis, Tennessee, by a white gunman; over the next four days race riots erupt in Chicago, Baltimore, Cincinnati, and Washington DC.

The Scourge of Violence

Much of Bobby Kennedy's political life was devoted to facing—and defeating—violence in its many forms. From his courageous stance against organized crime to his passionate defense of civil rights campaigners to his fervent opposition to the Vietnam War, he challenged practitioners of violence at every turn. His remarks on the topic can only serve to underline the terrible, tragic irony of its role in his own and his older brother's deaths.

"I thought they'd get one of us, but Jack, after all he's been through, never worried about it. I thought it would be me."

Following his brother's assassination

•

"Every society gets the kind of criminal it deserves. What is equally true is that every community gets the kind of law enforcement it insists on."

Attributed

•

"Whenever men take the law into their own hands, the loser is the law. And when the law loses, freedom languishes."

Day of Affirmation address

University of Capetown

June 6, 1966

•

"What is objectionable, what is dangerous about extremists, is not that they are extreme, but that they are intolerant. The evil is not what they say about their cause, but what they say about their opponents."

The Pursuit of Justice

———◈———

Bobby Kennedy was scheduled to give a speech to a predominantly African-American audience in Indianapolis when he learned that Dr. Martin Luther King Jr. had been assassinated. He set his speech aside and addressed the crowd ex temporaneously:

"Ladies and Gentlemen—I'm only going to talk to you just for a minute or so this evening. Because I have some very sad news for all of you, and I think sad news for all of our fellow citizens, and people who love peace all over the world, and that is that Martin Luther King was shot and was killed tonight in Memphis, Tennessee.

"For those of you who are black—considering the evidence is that there were white people who were responsible—you can be filled with bitterness, and with hatred, and a desire for revenge.

"We can move in that direction as a country, in greater polarization—black people amongst blacks, and white amongst whites, filled with hatred toward one another. Or we can make an effort, as Martin Luther King did, to understand and to comprehend, and replace that violence, that stain of bloodshed that has spread across our land, with an effort to understand compassion and love.

"For those of you who are black and are tempted to be filled with hatred and mistrust of the injustice of such an act, against all white people, I would only say that I can also feel in my own heart the same kind of feeling. I had a member of my family killed, but he was killed by a white man. . . .

"What we need in the United States is not division;

what we need in the United States is not hatred; what we need in the United States is not violence and lawlessness, but is love and wisdom, and compassion toward one another, and a feeling of justice toward those who still suffer within our country, whether they be white or whether they be black. . . .

"But the vast majority of white people and the vast majority of black people in this country want to live together, want to improve the quality of our life, and want justice for all human beings that abide in our land.

"Let us dedicate ourselves to what the Greeks wrote so many years ago: to tame the savageness of man and make gentle the life of this world. . . ."

April 4, 1968

One day after the assassination of Dr. King, Bobby gave a speech to the Cleveland City Club in Ohio on the mindless menace of violence:

"This is a time of shame and sorrow. It is not a day for politics. . . .

"It is not the concern of any one race. The victims of the violence are black and white, rich and poor, young and old, famous and unknown. They are, most important of all, human beings whom other human beings loved and needed. . . .

"What has violence ever accomplished? What has it ever created? No martyr's cause has ever been stilled by an assassin's bullet. . . . No wrongs have ever been righted by riots and civil disorders. A sniper is only a coward, not a hero; and an uncontrolled, uncontrollable mob is only the voice of madness, not the voice of reason. . . . Whenever any American's life is taken by another American unnecessarily—whether it is done in the name of the law or in defiance of the law, by one man or a gang, in cold blood or in passion, in an attack of violence or in response to violence—whenever we tear at the fabric of the life which another man has painfully and clumsily woven for himself and his children, the whole nation is degraded.

"'Among free men,' said Abraham Lincoln, 'there can be no successful appeal from the ballot to the bullet; and those who take such appeal are sure to lose their cause and pay the costs.' . . .

"Too often we honor swagger and bluster and the wielders of force; too often we excuse those who are willing to build their own lives on the shattered dreams of others. . . . Some look for scapegoats, others look for conspiracies, but this much is clear: violence breeds violence, repression brings retaliation, and only a cleaning of our whole society can remove this sickness from our soul. . . .

"We learn, at the last, to look at our brothers as aliens, men with whom we share a city, but not a community, men bound to us in common dwelling, but not in common effort. We learn to share only a common fear—only a common desire to retreat from each other—only a common impulse to meet disagreement with force. For all this there are no final answers. . . .

"Our lives on this planet are too short and the work to be done too great to let this spirit flourish any longer in our land. Of course we cannot vanish it with a program, nor with a resolution.

"But we can perhaps remember—even if only for a time—that those who live with us are our brothers, that they share with us the same short movement of life, that they seek—as we do—nothing but the chance to live out their lives in purpose and happiness, winning what satisfaction and fulfillment they can."

April 5, 1968

•

"Our brave young men are dying in the swamps of Southeast Asia. Which of them might have written a poem? Which of them might have cured cancer? Which of them might have played in a World Series or given us the gift of laughter from the stage or helped build a bridge or a university? Which of them would have taught a child to read? It is our responsibility to let these men live. . . . It is indecent if they die because of the empty vanity of their country."

Vietnam War speech

California

March 24, 1968

.

"The advice 'bomb them back to the Stone Age' may show that the speaker is already there himself. But it could, if followed, force all of us to join him."

Attributed

———◦◉◦———

President Johnson traveled in an armored limousine behind a screen of bulletproof glass. Bobby gave his opinion on that vehicle to a reporter early in his own presidential campaign:

"I'll tell you one thing: if I'm elected President, you won't find me riding around in any of those God-damned cars. We can't have that kind of country, where the President is afraid to go among the people."

•

"Are we like the God of the Old Testament that we can decide, in Washington DC, what cities, what towns, what hamlets in Vietnam are going to be destroyed? . . . Do we have to accept that? . . . I do not think we have to. I think we can do something about it."

Final Senate speech, on Vietnam

Citizenship and Civil Rights

"On this generation of Americans falls the burden of proving to the world that we really mean it when we say all men are created free and are equal before the law. All of us might wish at times that we lived in a more tranquil world, but we don't. And if our times are difficult and perplexing, so are they challenging, and filled with opportunity."

Speech at University of Georgia Law School

May 6, 1961

•

"Since the days of Greece and Rome when the word 'citizen' was a title of honor, we have often seen more emphasis put on the rights of citizenship than on its responsibilities. And today, as never before in the free world, responsibility is the greatest right of citizenship and service is the greatest of freedom's privileges."

Speech at University of San Francisco Law School

September 29, 1962

•

"Nations, like men, often march to the beat of different drummers, and the precise solutions of the United States can neither be dictated nor transplanted to others. What is important is that all nations must march toward an increasing freedom; toward justice for all; toward a society strong and flexible enough to meet the demands of all of its own people, and a world of immense and dizzying change. . . .

"We must recognize the full human equality of all our people—before God, before the law, and in the councils of government. We must do this not because it is economically advantageous—although it is; not because the laws of God and man command it—although they do command it; not because people in other lands wish it so. We must do it for the single and fundamental reason that it is the right thing to do."

Day of Affirmation address

University of Capetown

June 6, 1966

•

"Democracy is no easy form of government. Few nations have been able to sustain it. For it requires that we take the chances of freedom; that the liberating play of reason be brought to bear on events filled with passion; that dissent be allowed to make its appeal for acceptance; that men chance error in their search for truth."

Vietnam War speech

February 19, 1966

⸺◈⸺

Bobby delivered a famous campaign speech to the then all-white student body at Creighton University in Omaha, Nebraska. He asked them challenging questions and was booed.

"Look around you. How many black faces do you see here? How many American Indians? The fact is, if you look at any regiment or division of paratroopers in Vietnam, forty-five percent of them are black. How can you accept this?"

May 13, 1968

•

"President Kennedy's favorite quote was really from Dante, 'The hottest places in Hell are reserved for those who in time of moral crisis preserve their neutrality.'"

Columbia University / Barnard Democratic Club

October 5, 1964

•

"The sharpest criticism often goes hand in hand with the deepest idealism and love of country."

Philadelphia, Pennsylvania

February 24, 1967

The following is an excerpt from the last speech of Bobby Kennedy's life:

"I think we can end the divisions within the United States. What I think is quite clear is that we can work together in the last analysis, and that what has been going on in the United States over the period of the last three years, the violence, the disenchantment with our society, the divisions—whether between blacks and whites, between the poor and the more affluent, or between age groups, or in the war in Vietnam—that we

can work together. We are a great country, and an unselfish country, and a compassionate country. And I
intend to make that my basis for running."

Victory speech following California primary election

June 4, 1968

•

"And as long as America must choose, that long will
there be a need and a place for the Democratic Party.
We Democrats can run on our record but we cannot
rest on it. We will win if we continue to take the initiative and if we carry the message of hope and action
throughout the country. Alexander Smith once said, 'A
man doesn't plant a tree for himself. He plants it for pos-
terity.' Let us continue to plant, and our children shall
reap the harvest. That is our destiny as Democrats."

Speech at testimonial dinner for Lieutenant Governor

Patrick J. Lucey

Madison, Wisconsin

August 15, 1965

A Too-Brief Campaign

On March 16, 1968, Bobby Kennedy went to the caucus room of the Old Senate Office Building to announce his candidacy for the presidency. His brother had made his own campaign announcement in the same room, and Bobby began with the same words JFK had used.

"I am announcing today my candidacy for the presidency of the United States. . . . I am running to close the gaps that now exist between black and white, between rich and poor, between young and old. . . .

"I do not lightly dismiss the dangers and the difficulties of challenging an incumbent president. But these are not ordinary times and this is not an ordinary election. At stake is not simply the leadership of our party and even our country. It is our right to the moral leadership of this planet."

.

"Some men see things as they are and say, 'Why?' I dream of things that never were and say, 'Why not?'"

These words became a centerpiece of Bobby's presidential campaign in 1968, and he repeated them on several occasions, using them as a kind of literary slogan. The quotation, which originates from the mouth of the serpent in George Bernard Shaw's play Back to Methuselah, *was also used by JFK when he addressed the Irish parliament in 1963.*

.

"If we fail to dare, if we do not try, the next generation will harvest the fruit of our indifference; a world we did not want—a world we did not choose—but a world we could have made better, by caring more for the results of our labors. And we shall be left only with the hollow apology of T. S. Eliot: 'That is not what I meant at all. That is not it, at all.' "

Speech at Americana Hotel

New York City, New York

August 23, 1967

•

"Some of you may not like what you're going to hear in a few minutes, but it's what I believe; and if I'm elected President, it's what I'm going to do . . ."

Remarks shortly before first campaign speech

University of Kansas student union

March 18, 1968

•

"Too much and too long, we seem to have surrendered community excellence and community values in the mere accumulation of material things. Our gross national product . . . if we should judge America by that—counts air pollution and cigarette advertising, and ambulances to clear our highways of carnage. It counts special locks for our doors and the jails for those who break them. It counts the destruction of our redwoods and the loss of our natural wonder in chaotic sprawl. It counts napalm and the cost of a nuclear warhead, and armored cars for police who fight riots in our streets. It counts Whitman's rifle and Speck's knife, and the television programs which glorify violence in order to sell toys to our children.

"Yet the gross national product does not allow for the health of our children, the quality of their education, or the joy of their play. It does not include the beauty of our poetry or the strength of our marriages; the intelligence of our public debate or the integrity of our public officials. It measures neither our wit nor our courage; neither our wisdom nor our learning; neither our compassion nor our devotion to our country; it measures everything, in short, except that which makes life worthwhile. And it tells us everything about America except why we are proud that we are Americans. . . .

"Our country is in danger: not just from foreign enemies; but above all, from our own misguided policies—and what they can do to the nation that Thomas Jefferson once said was the last, great hope of mankind. There is a contest on, not for the rule of America but for the heart of America. In these next eight months we are going to decide what this country will stand for—and what kind of men we are."

First campaign speech
University of Kansas
March 18, 1968

•

"If we don't get out of this war, I don't know what these young people are going to do."

Remark to reporters during the presidential campaign

When asked if he would support Johnson if LBJ won the party's nomination for president in 1968, Bobby replied that he had "grave reservations" about the president. He continued:

"I'm loyal to the Democratic Party, but I feel stronger about the United States and mankind generally."

Meet the Press

March 17, 1968

·

"I didn't want to run for president. But when [Johnson] made it clear the war would go on, and that nothing was going to change, I had no choice."

On the first flight of his campaign aircraft

————◆————

When his aides urged him to make fewer personal appearances and rely more on television to get his message across, Bobby rejected that advice with this rationale:

"There are so many people who hate me that I've got to let the people who love me see me. . . .

"For every two or three days that you waste time making speeches at rallies full of noise and balloons, there's usually a chance every two or three days . . . where you get a chance to teach people something; and to tell them something that they don't know because they don't have the chance to get around like I do, to take them some place vicariously that they haven't been, to show them a ghetto or an Indian reservation."

Inspirational Remarks

"The future is not a gift: it is an achievement. Every generation helps make its own future. This is the essential challenge of the present."

Speech at Seattle World's Fair

August 7, 1962

•

"All great questions must be raised by great voices, and the greatest voice is the voice of the people—speaking out—in prose, or painting or poetry or music; speaking out—in homes and halls, streets and farms, courts and cafes—let that voice speak and the stillness you hear will be the gratitude of mankind."

Speech in New York City, New York

January 22, 1963

•

"I believe that, as long as there is plenty, poverty is evil."

Speech in Athens, Georgia

May 6, 1961

•

"Our future may lie beyond our vision, but it is not completely beyond our control. It is the shaping impulse of America that neither fate nor nature nor the irresistible tides of history, but the work of our own hands, matched to reason and principle, that will determine our destiny. There is pride in that, even arrogance, but there is also experiences and truth. In any event, it is the only way we can live.

"This world demands the qualities of youth: not a time of life but a state of mind, a temper of the will, a quality of imagination, a predominance of courage over timidity, of the appetite for adventure over the life of ease. . . .

"Only those who dare to fail greatly, can ever achieve greatly."

Day of Affirmation address

University of Capetown

June 6, 1966

•

"The future does not belong to those who are content with today, apathetic toward common problems and their fellow man alike, timid and fearful in the face of bold projects and new ideas. Rather, it will belong to those who can blend passion, reason and courage in a personal commitment to the great enterprises and ideals of American society."

Speech at University of California, Berkeley

October 22, 1966

Wit

The famous Kennedy humor was present in Bobby in good measure. A number of his remarks were captured for attribution by friends, reporters, and associates.

"I was sick last year, and my friends in the Senate sent me a get-well card. The vote was 42 to 41."

Attributed

•

"I'm glad to come to the University of Alabama. I'm delighted to see the inside of this building. I didn't think it meant anything that they snuck me around the back way."

March 21, 1968

•

"I was the seventh of nine children. When you come from that far down, you have to struggle to survive."

Attributed

•

"He knows all the facts, and he's against all the solutions."

Comment on Senator Daniel Patrick Moynihan

•

"Fear not the path of truth for the lack of people walking on it."

Victory speech following California primary election

June 4, 1968

•

"My views on birth control are somewhat distorted by the fact that I was the seventh of nine children."

Attributed

•

"When Mister Khrushchev reported that the cosmonauts—like the Bolshevik pilots of the early twenties—reported seeing 'no signs of God' we can only suggest that they aim, with the rest of mankind, a little higher."

Attributed

——◦——

Bobby's relationship with his brother's vice president, Lyndon Johnson, was not warm. It became even more contentious when Johnson became president following JFK's assassination, though Bobby did continue to serve as attorney general until just before the 1964 election. Afterward, he made several pointed remarks about Johnson.

"How do you tell if Lyndon is lying? If he wiggles his ears, that doesn't mean he's lying. If he raises his eyebrows, that doesn't mean he's lying. But when he moves his lips, he's lying."

•

"President Johnson once said to me, 'Go west, young man.' I thought he was trying to tell me something, because I was in California at the time."

———◦◉◦———

When a youngster asked Bobby if he took good care of his children, he replied:

"I asked my children and they voted 'yes,' by four to three, with two abstentions."

•

"People say I am ruthless. I am not ruthless. And if I find the man who called me ruthless, I shall destroy him."

Attributed

•

"I have a speech which it is my responsibility to give, and you have a responsibility to listen to it. And if you finish before I do, let me know."

University of Kansas (to a student audience)

March 18, 1968

•

"One fifth of the people are against everything all the time."

Attributed

—◦◦◦—

Bobby's personal and political lives, like those all of the Kennedys, were partially defined by his Roman Catholic faith. Still, Bobby was known to be slightly irreverent on occasion.

"The mother superior said she had been praying to Saint Jude for me. I thanked her, then asked somebody who Saint Jude was. I learned that he is the patron saint of impossible causes."

Attributed

•

"We had a friendly audience with Pope John. He blessed us all, including the American newspapermen who were traveling with us, most of whom were not

Catholics. He assured them that it was just a little blessing and wouldn't do them any harm."

Attributed

•

"We spent part of our honeymoon here and have had ten children since, so I guess I learned something!"

To a group of students

Brigham Young University

•

"Thomas Jefferson once said that he cared not who made a country's laws, so long as he could write its newspapers. If this Congress goes on much longer, I'd rather be in the newspaper business too."

Attributed

About Bobby

"Perhaps we cannot prevent this world from being a world in which children are tortured. But we can reduce the number of tortured children. And if you don't help us, who else in the world can help us do this?"

Albert Camus dedication to

To Seek a Newer World, by Robert F. Kennedy

.

"What he did was not really that mystical. All it requires is someone who knows himself and has some courage."

Presidential-campaign aide, after RFK's assassination

.

"He named excellent men to most key posts, put new vigor into protecting civil rights through administrative action, [and] played a pivotal role in shaping the most comprehensive civil rights law in this country."

The New York Times

on Bobby's tenure as attorney general

.

"Oh God! It can't happen to this family again!"

Anguished bystander

Ambassador Hotel

June 5, 1968

.

"I knew him only as an icon. In that sense, it is a distance I share with most of the people who now work in this Capitol—many of whom were not even born when Bobby Kennedy died. But what's interesting is that if you go throughout the offices in the Capitol, everywhere you'll find photographs of Kennedy, or collections of his speeches, or some other memento of his life. . . .

"If he were here today, I think it would be hard to place Robert F. Kennedy into any of the categories that so often constrain us politically. He was a fervent anti-communist but knew diplomacy was our way out of the Cuban Missile Crisis. He sought to wage the war on poverty but with local partnerships and community activism. He was at once both hardheaded and big-hearted.

"And yet, his was not a centrism in the sense of finding a middle road or a certain point on the ideological spectrum. His was a politics that, at its heart, was deeply moral—based on the notion that in this world, there is right and there is wrong, and it's our job to organize our laws and our lives around recognizing the difference. . . ."

Senator Barack Obama

Robert F. Kennedy Human Rights Award Ceremony

Washington DC

November 16, 2005

Eulogy

In a tragic mirroring of Bobby's eloquent speech about his older brother, Teddy Kennedy, too, was put in the position of eulogizing a brother who was also an American icon, also slain by an assassin. He spoke at Bobby's funeral:

"We loved him as a brother, and as a father, and as a son. . . . He gave us strength in time of trouble, wisdom in time of uncertainty, and sharing in time of happiness. He will always be by our side.

"Love is not an easy feeling to put into words. Nor is loyalty, or trust, or joy. But he was all of these. He loved life completely and he lived it intensely.

"A few years back, Robert Kennedy wrote some words about his own father which express the way we in his family felt about him. He said of what his father meant to him, and I quote: 'What it really all adds up to is love—not love as it is described with such facility in popular magazines, but the kind of love that is affection and respect, order and encouragement, and support. Our awareness of this was an incalculable source of strength, and because real love is something unselfish and involves sacrifice and giving, we could not help but profit from it.'

"And he continued, 'Beneath it all, he has tried to engender a social conscience. There were wrongs which needed attention. There were people who were poor and needed help. And we have a responsibility to them and to this country. Through no virtues and accomplishments of our own, we have been fortunate enough to be born in the United States under the most comfortable conditions. We, therefore, have a responsibility to others who are less well off.'

"That is what Robert Kennedy was given. What he leaves to us is what he said, what he did, and what he stood for. . . . Few will have the greatness to bend history itself, but each of us can work to change a small portion of events, and in the total of all those acts will be written the history of this generation. . . . Few are willing to brave the disapproval of their fellows, the censure of their colleagues, the wrath of their society. Moral courage is a rarer commodity than bravery in battle or great intelligence. Yet it is the one essential, vital quality for those who seek to change a world that yields most painfully to change. And I believe that in this generation those with the courage to enter the moral conflict will find themselves with companions in every corner of the globe.

"For the fortunate among us, there is the temptation to follow the easy and familiar paths of personal ambition and financial success so grandly spread before those who enjoy the privilege of education. But that is not the road history has marked out for us. Like it or not, we live in times of danger and uncertainty. But they are also more open to the creative energy of men than any other time in history. All of us will ultimately be judged, and as the years pass we will surely judge ourselves on the effort we have contributed to building a new world society and the extent to which our ideals and goals have shaped that event. . . .

"That is the way he lived. That is what he leaves us.

"My brother need not be idealized, or enlarged in death beyond what he was in life; to be remembered simply as a good and decent man, who saw wrong and tried to right it, saw suffering and tried to heal it, saw war and tried to stop it."

EDWARD MOORE KENNEDY

"Teddy"

February 22, 1932–August 25, 2009

The work goes on, the cause endures, the hope still lives, and the dream shall never die.

SENATOR EDWARD KENNEDY
DEMOCRATIC NATIONAL CONVENTION
NEW YORK CITY, NEW YORK
AUGUST 12, 1980

A s the youngest of Joseph and Rosemary Kennedy's nine children, Teddy spent his early years with, perhaps, a little less of the pressure to succeed than was placed on the shoulders of his older brothers. He was happy and carefree as a child, doted on by his older siblings. But life in his family had a way of bringing even the youngsters face-to-face with cold reality: Teddy was only twelve when he learned that his oldest brother, Joe Jr., had been killed flying a combat mission in World War II.

Teddy, the youngest member of a large and active family, moved a lot during his early years, attending ten different schools by the time he was twelve. He had been born in Boston, but during these years Teddy lived in Bronxville, New York; Hyannis Port, Massachusetts; Palm Beach, Florida; and even London, England. When he was seven years old, he received his first communion from Pope Pius XII in Rome.

Teddy was not quite the scholar that Jack and

Bobby proved to be, though he performed adequately at school and was quite successful at football. In 1950 he enrolled at Harvard University but enlisted in the United States Army in June 1951. Honorably discharged in March, 1953, he reenrolled in Harvard that summer and was more successful academically; he also continued to play football.

He graduated from Harvard in 1956 and immediately enrolled in the University of Virginia Law School, where he proceeded to win the William Minor Lile Moot Court competition. He studied at the Hague Academy of International Law during 1958 but returned to manage his brother Jack's Senate reelection campaign. His affable and easygoing nature helped his brother win in a historic landslide. Afterward, Ted finished his law degree and was admitted to the Massachusetts Bar Association (in 1959).

On November 29, 1958, he married Virginia Joan Bennett. The couple would go on to have three children, Kara Anne (b. February 27, 1960), Edward Jr. (b. September 26, 1961), and Patrick (b. July 14, 1967).

In the meantime, Teddy began his political career. He managed JFK's presidential campaign in the West, earning his pilot's license and flying tirelessly from one campaign stop to another. He spent nearly two months in Wisconsin, where Jack scored a major primary victory over Hubert Humphrey, the senator from neighboring Minnesota.

Following his brother's electoral victory, Teddy began a legal career as an assistant district attorney in Massachusetts. But politics was in his blood, and as soon as he was old enough (thirty) he ran in a special election for the United States Senate seat from Massachusetts formerly held by his brother. He defeated the state's attorney general in a hard-fought primary, and then defeated a formidable Republican opponent, George Cabot Lodge II, in a November 1962 special election.

Only a year later, Jack was assassinated in Dallas. Teddy had the grim duty of traveling to Hyannis Port to give the awful news to their father, who had suffered a serious stroke in 1961. A year later, Ted and fellow senator Birch Bayh II survived an airplane crash in which the pilot and one of Teddy's aides were killed. Bayh heroically dragged him from the wreckage, though Senator Kennedy suffered a broken back and other injuries. Nonetheless his wife ran the campaign for the hospitalized senator, and Kennedy won his seat in the 1964 regular election, garnering some seventy-five percent of the votes. By 1965 he was back in the Senate, although walking with a cane, and he began to establish the reputation as a liberal champion in the Kennedy tradition. He worked hard to get a ban on the poll tax added to the Voting Rights Act and played a major role in gaining passage of the Immigration and Nationality Act.

He was also increasingly leery of the dangers posed

by America's growing involvement in the Vietnam War. Although he was not at first enthusiastic about Bobby's decision to run for the presidency in 1968, Teddy came around because of the strong antiwar beliefs they both possessed. When Bobby announced his campaign, Ted served in the same role he did for Jack, campaigning in the western states. Thus, he was in San Francisco when Bobby was shot and fatally wounded in Los Angeles.

Deeply grieving over this second assassination, Ted rejected all attempts to draft him as a candidate in his brother's place. Though he remained in the Senate, he also became the patriarch of his family and assumed an important role in the lives of all of Jack's and Bobby's children.

Although he was elected to the influential Senate majority whip position in January of 1969—the youngest ever to hold that role—Teddy did not feel ready to make a run at the Oval Office. Instead, he was reelected to his Senate seat in 1970 and continued to serve in that august body, where he was steadily polishing his political skills. Despite a clamor of support, he declined to pursue the presidency in 1972, instead pushing hard for the Federal Election Campaign Act Amendment, which passed in 1974.

In 1976, again, Kennedy declined to run, and Jimmy Carter won the Democratic nomination and then the presidency. Kennedy and Carter were the two most powerful Democrats in Washington during the next four years, but they were not close, and in fact Ted was frustrated by Carter's unwillingness to work toward Kennedy's most important goal, a system of national health insurance. Teddy did make successful trips to both China and the Soviet Union during this period and became chairman of the powerful Senate Judiciary Committee in 1978.

By August, 1979, Kennedy had decided the time was right to run for president in the 1980 election, even though it would mean challenging a Democratic incumbent. He mounted a serious challenge against Carter, but when the Iranian hostage crisis began on November 4, the nation rallied around the sitting commander-in-chief. Kennedy won several primaries, but he lost more of them, and when the party moved to its convention in New York City, during August, he finally withdrew and yielded the nomination to Carter.

In January 1981, Teddy and Joan divorced. That same month, Ronald Reagan became president and the Republicans assumed control of the Senate. With several of his Democratic colleagues now out of office, Teddy Kennedy found himself as the primary champion of liberal policies at the top of the United States government. Throughout the decade he worked endlessly to support women's issues, civil rights, gay rights, and other progressive causes. He became adept at forming alliances with influential Republican senators, and several of them—Utah's Orrin Hatch being the most notable—became Teddy's good friends.

When Ted easily won reelection in 1982, he was given the unusual privilege of a seat on a third major committee, the Armed Services Committee. From this pulpit he resisted many of President Reagan's foreign policies, including interventions in El Salvador and Nicaragua, and weapons systems such as the B1 bomber and the hugely expensive "Star Wars" missile-defense system. He also visited South Africa in 1985, ignoring the wishes of the apartheid government by personally meeting with Bishop Desmond Tutu and Winnie Mandela (whose husband, Nelson Mandela, was in prison). Following his visit he led the charge for economic sanctions against South Africa and gathered enough votes to override President Reagan's veto of the sanction legislation.

In 1986 Democrats regained control of the Senate, and Kennedy became chairman of the Labor and

Public Welfare Committee. His most influential role in the 1980s came through his place on the Judiciary Committee, however, when he led the fight to block Reagan's choice of Robert Bork's appointment to the Supreme Court. Bork's haughty disdain for Kennedy's position did the judge no favors, and in a surprising upset the committee and the full Senate rejected his appointment. In 1988, Kennedy sailed through his re-election with the largest victory margin of his life.

In June 1991, Kennedy began dating Victoria Reggie, a Washington lawyer and the daughter of an old family friend. They were married on July 3, 1992, and she became Teddy's soul mate and partner. With his presidential aspirations contentedly behind him, Ted Kennedy settled into his destiny as the "liberal lion of the Senate." He comfortably won reelection in 1994, 2000, and 2006. In April 2006, *Time* magazine selected him as one of America's top-ten senators.

Senator Kennedy and his wife were the proud

owners of two Portuguese water dogs, and in 2006 Teddy wrote a children's book called *My Senator and Me: A Dog's Eye View of Washington D.C.* (In 2009 Ted and Victoria would be instrumental in finding a dog of the same breed for President Barack Obama's family.) Teddy authored another book published in 2006, a political history titled *America Back on Track*.

After more than a year of courageously battling brain cancer, during which time he still worked vigorously toward his goal of universal health care for Americans, Ted Kennedy finally succumbed to the disease on August 25, 2009.

———◆———

"Our progressive vision is not just for Democrats or Republicans, for red states and blue states. It's a way forward for the nation as a whole to a new prosperity and greater opportunity for all; a vision not just of the country we *can* become, but the country we *must* become: an America that embraces the values and aspirations of our people now and for coming generations."

Speech on the future of the Democratic Party

January 12, 2005

Timeline — Rising into a New Century

August 29, 1968 The Democratic National Convention in Chicago is marred by riots and police brutality as Hubert H. Humphrey is nominated to face Richard Nixon in November.

November 6, 1968 Richard Nixon wins the presidency in a close election; the Democrat Shirley Chisholm wins the 12th Congressional District seat in the House of Representatives, becoming the first African-American woman in Congress.

July 20, 1969 Neal Armstrong becomes the first man to walk on the moon, where he plants an American flag.

April 30, 1970 President Nixon orders American combat troops into Cambodia in an effort to destroy Vietcong and North Vietnamese military bases and supply routes.

August 25, 1971 A new round of violence breaks out in Northern Ireland, as British troops clash with the Irish Republican Army (IRA). Some two dozen people are killed, and much of Belfast is in ruins.

June 17, 1972 Five burglars are arrested in the offices of the Democratic National Committee, in the Watergate Building, in Washington DC.

August 11, 1972 The last American combat unit pulls out of South Vietnam.

November 8, 1972 Nixon defeats Senator George McGovern in a landslide to win a second term as president.

December, 1973 The twin towers of the World Trade Center are completed in New York City, becoming a dominant feature of the Manhattan skyline.

August 8, 1974 Richard Nixon, fully implicated in the Watergate scandal and facing impeachment, becomes the first president to resign the office; Vice President Gerald Ford assumes the presidency.

April 30, 1975 The fall of Saigon marks the end of the Vietnam War, as Communist forces now control the whole country.

November 2, 1976 Jimmy Carter defeats Gerald Ford in a close presidential election.

September 18, 1978 President Carter, the Egyptian president Anwar Sadat, and the Israeli prime minister Menachem Begin achieve a potentially historic peace agreement after meeting at Camp David, Maryland.

November 26, 1979 Following the Iranian Revolution, during which Ayatollah Khomeini's fundamentalist radicals took over the country, students seize the American embassy in Tehran and take fifty-two American hostages.

November 4, 1980 Ronald Reagan defeats Jimmy Carter to become, at sixty-nine, the oldest man ever elected president.

January 31, 1981 The fifty-two Iranian hostages are finally released and arrive home after 444 days of captivity.

April 14, 1981 The space shuttle *Columbia* completes its maiden voyage, becoming the world's first reusable spacecraft.

October 6, 1981 Anwar Sadat is assassinated by fundamentalist rebels from his own country.

March 23, 1983 President Reagan announces the Strategic Defense Initiative, an as-yet-theoretical space-based system designed to destroy incoming ballistic missiles; the program is commonly known as "Star Wars."

November 6, 1984 President Reagan and Vice President George Bush win a landslide election over Democrat Walter Mondale and his running mate, Geraldine Ferraro—the first woman on a major-party ticket in a presidential campaign.

January 31, 1986 The space shuttle *Challenger* explodes shortly after liftoff, killing all seven on board.

November 8, 1988 George H. W. Bush defeats Michael Dukakis to continue the Republican control of the White House.

November 9, 1989 The Berlin wall is torn open as the Communist Bloc crumbles all across Eastern Europe, replaced in most nations with neophyte democracies.

February 28, 1991 The Gulf War ends when American forces, together with numerous allies, win a stunning victory in Operation Desert Storm, driving out the Iraqi forces that had invaded Kuwait the previous year.

November 3, 1992 Bill Clinton is elected president, defeating George H. W. Bush and the billionaire-populist Ross Perot (who won eighteen percent of the vote).

November, 1994 Republicans gain control of both the House and the Senate for the first time since 1955.

November 4, 1995 The Israeli prime minister, Yitzhak Rabin, is assassinated by a fundamentalist from his own country.

November 5, 1996 President Clinton wins reelection by a substantial margin over the Republican challenger, Bob Dole.

August 7, 1998 Hundreds are killed when terrorists supported by Osama bin Laden bomb American embassies in Kenya and Tanzania.

November 7, 2000 George W. Bush defeats Al Gore in the closest presidential election in US history (with a margin of barely five hundred controversial votes cast in the decisive state of Florida).

September 11, 2001 Osama bin Laden's Al Qaeda terrorists hijack four planes and kill nearly 3,000 victims in the deadliest foreign attack ever to occur on American soil; the World Trade Center is destroyed.

March 20, 2003 The US invades Iraq, ostensibly because the Iraqi president, Saddam Hussein, is stockpiling weapons of mass destruction.

November 2, 2004 George W. Bush defeats John Kerry to win reelection.

November, 2006 Democrats win majorities in both the House and Senate.

November 4, 2008 Barack Obama defeats Senator John McCain to become the first African-American elected president.

The Patriarch

"The disadvantage of my position is constantly being compared to brothers of such superior ability."

After JFK became president

*

"I believe that each of us as individuals must not only struggle to make a better world, but to make ourselves better, too. [Unlike my brothers] I have been given length of years and time. And as I approach my 60th birthday, I am determined to give all that I have to advance the causes for which I have stood for almost a quarter of a century."

Speech at the JFK School of Government,

Institute of Politics

October 25, 1991

After JFK's assassination, Jacqueline Kennedy helped create the Camelot imagery of her husband's administration. For the rest of her life, even though she remarried, she maintained close ties with the Kennedy clan. When she passed away in 1994, Ted described her importance to the family at her funeral:

"She was always there for our family in her special way. She was a blessing to us and to the nation—and a lesson to the world on how to do things right, how to be a mother, how to appreciate history, how to be courageous. No one else looked like her, spoke like her, wrote like her, or was so original in the way she did things. No one we knew ever had a better sense of self. . . .

"No one ever gave more meaning to the title of 'First Lady. . . .'

"And then, during those four endless days in 1963, she held us together as a family and a country. In large part because of her, we could grieve and then go on. She lifted us up, and in the doubt and darkness, she gave her fellow citizens back their pride as Americans. She was then 34 years old. . . .

"She made a rare and noble contribution to the American spirit. But for us, most of all she was a magnificent wife, a mother, a grandmother, a sister, aunt, and friend.

"She graced our history. And for those of us who knew and loved her—she graced our lives."

May 24, 1994

•

"I don't think that there's any question that my relationship with Vicki has had a very profound, welcome, happy impact."

Announcement of his engagement

September 7, 1992

•

"She did everything nine times. And now she's doing everything 29 times again. For half a century, she has been gently stretching each child and grandchild toward her goal of excellence."

Speaking about his mother

Georgetown University

1977

•

"It is obvious that she had instilled in the next generation the enduring bonds of love and faith that tie us together as a family."

Foreword to *Her Grace Above Gold*,

a collection of essays about Rose Kennedy

When his nephew, and President Kennedy's only son, perished in a plane crash, tragedy once again thrust Ted into the role of family spokesman.

"From the first day of his life, John seemed to belong not only to our family, but to the American family. The whole world knew his name before he did. . . .

"We dared to think, in that other Irish phrase, that this John Kennedy would live to comb gray hair, with his beloved Carolyn by his side. But like his father, he had every gift of life but length of years."

Tribute to John F. Kennedy Jr.

July 23, 1999

•

"You try to live with the upside and the . . . happier aspects and the joyous aspects, and try to muffle the other kinds of concerns and anxiety and the sadness of it, and know that you have no alternative but to continue on.

"And so you do."

CBS News, *60 Minutes*,

Gloria Berger interview with Caroline Kennedy

and Ted Kennedy,

May 2, 2000

•

"The best time to visit Arlington [National Cemetery] is in the morning. That's when I visit. It's cooler, and the crowds aren't there yet."

Brian and Alma Hart, interview by Don Aucoin,

July 16, 2008, as reported in

The Last Lion: The Fall and Rise of Ted Kennedy

————◦❖◦————

On every anniversary of the 9/11 terrorist attacks, Teddy contacted each of the families of the victims from Massachu-

setts. He sent the following note to Christie Coombs, whose husband was killed that day.

"Dear Christie, Vicki and I wanted you to know that we are thinking of you and your entire family during this difficult time of the year. As you know so well, the passage of time never really heals the tragic memory of such a great loss, but we carry on, because we have to, because our loved one would want us to, and because there is still light to guide us in the world from the love they gave us."

September 11, 2005

The Liberal Lion

It wasn't until Ted Kennedy grew completely comfortable in his role as a senator than he could truly take his proper place on the nation's political stage.

"I know this decision means I may never be president. But the pursuit of the presidency is not my life. Public service is."

Statement that he would not run in 1988

December 1985

———◦◦◦———

Teddy grew increasingly displeased with Jimmy Carter's leadership in the late 1970s. He chided the president with increasingly pointed remarks and notably used the imagery of one of his favorite pastimes:

"Sometimes a party must sail against the wind. We cannot afford to drift or lie at anchor. We cannot heed the call of those who say it is time to furl the sail."

Speech at the Democratic mid-term convention

Memphis, Tennessee

December 1978

•

"Integrity is the lifeblood of democracy. Deceit is a poison in its veins."

Attributed

•

"I believe we must not permit the dream of social progress to be shattered by those whose premises have failed."

Speech at Georgetown University

February 1980

•

"The conquest of cancer is a special problem of such enormous concern to all Americans. I think every one of us in this body, and most families across the country, have been touched by this disease one way or the other."

Senate speech before the passage of the

cancer bill he sponsored

1971

When Senator Kennedy received a mass mailing inviting him to join the conservative group Moral Majority, he was amused to find himself listed among the dangerous individuals opposed by the group. He contacted the Reverend Jerry Falwell, the group's founder, and Teddy soon found himself delivering a speech at Liberty Baptist College, a school that Falwell had founded and still supervised.

"A number of people in Washington were surprised that I was invited to speak here—and even more surprised when I accepted the invitation. They seem to think that it's easier for a camel to pass through the eye of the needle than for a Kennedy to come to the campus of Liberty Baptist College. . . .

"I realize that my visit may be a little controversial. But as many of you have heard, Dr. Falwell recently sent me a membership in the Moral Majority—and I didn't even apply for it. . . ."

Teddy went on to discuss the idea of a freeze of nuclear weapons, which was a contentious topic during the Reagan years:

"There is no morality in the mushroom cloud. The black rain of nuclear ashes will fall alike on the just and the unjust. And then it will be too late to wish that we had done the real work of this atomic age—which is to seek a world that is neither red nor dead. . . .

"And it does not advance the debate to contend that the arms race is more divine punishment than human problem, or that in any event, the final days are near. As Pope John said two decades ago, at the opening of the Second Vatican Council: 'We must beware of those who burn with zeal, but are not endowed with much sense . . . we must disagree with the prophets of doom, who are always forecasting disasters, as though the end of the earth was at hand.' . . .

"I hope for an America where we can all contend freely and vigorously, but where we will treasure and guard those standards of civility which alone make this nation safe for both democracy and diversity. . . .

"I believe it is possible; the choice lies within us; as fellow citizens, let us live peaceably with each other; as fellow human beings, let us strive to live peaceably with men and women everywhere. Let that be our purpose and our prayer, yours and mine—for ourselves, for our country, and for all the world."

October 3, 1983

When President Reagan announced the nomination of the aloof, imperious, and ever-so-conservative judge Robert Bork to the United States Supreme Court, Ted Kennedy led the charge, ultimately successfully, in fighting that nomination.

"Robert Bork's America is a land in which women would be forced into back alley abortions, blacks would sit at segregated lunch counters, rogue police could break down citizens' doors in midnight raids, schoolchildren could not be taught about evolution, writers and artists could be censored at the whim of government, and the doors of the federal courts would be shut on the fingers of millions of citizens for whom the judiciary is often the only protector of the individual rights that are at the heart of our democracy. America is a better and freer nation than Robert Bork thinks. Yet in the current delicate balance of the Supreme Court, his rigid ideology will tip the scales of justice against the kind of country America is and ought to be."

Senate speech

July 1, 1987

•

"You want to yell at someone? You yell at me, Sununu! You don't yell at our staff. You don't treat our staff that way."

To John Sununu, chief of staff to

President George H. W. Bush

Meeting on the Americans with Disabilities Act

1990

•

"As of today, many questions still remain unanswered: Is war the only option? How much support will we have from the international community? How will war affect our global war against terrorism? How long will the United States need to stay in Iraq? How many casualties will there be?"

To Defense Secretary Donald Rumsfeld

Senate Armed Services Committee hearing

September 19, 2002

•

"The power to declare war is the most solemn responsibility given to Congress by the Constitution. We must not delegate that responsibility to the President in advance."

Explaining his no vote on the Iraq War Resolution

October 11, 2002

The measure passed the Senate with 77 yea votes.

———◦◉◦———

Ted met Brian and Alma Hart at their son's funeral at Ar-
lington National Cemetery. John Hart had been killed in
Iraq by a roadside bomb while riding in a Humvee that
lacked armored protection. Together, the Harts and Teddy
campaigned for better equipment to protect our soldiers.

"The number one priority of the Department of Defense this year should be to supply our troops with all
the protection they need to get the job done and re-
turn safely home."

Ted Kennedy, Brian Hart, and Alma Hart

Boston Globe opinion piece

February 3, 2005

Senator Kennedy also led the fight against President George W. Bush's most extreme judicial nominations, and Teddy's eloquent efforts stopped several crucial appointments.

"President Bush has said he wants judges who will follow the law, not try to re-write it. But his actions tell a different story. The contested nominees have records that make clear they would push the agenda of a narrow far right fringe, rather than protect rights important to all Americans.

"Priscilla Owen, Janice Rogers Brown, [and] William Myers . . . would erase much of the country's hard-fought progress toward equality and opportunity. Their values — favoring big business over the needs of families, destroying environmental protections, and turning back the clock on civil rights — are not mainstream values.

"As a Texas Supreme Court Justice, Priscilla Owen has shown clear hostility to fundamental rights, particularly on issues of major importance to workers, consumers, victims of discrimination, and women. Neither the facts, nor the law, nor established legal precedents, stop her from reaching her desired result.

"Even many newspapers that endorsed her campaign for the Texas Supreme Court now oppose her confirmation after seeing how poorly she served as a judge. *The Houston Chronicle* wrote that Justice Owen 'too often contorts rulings to conform to her particular conservative outlook.' The paper also noted that 'It's saying something that Owen is a regular dissenter on a Texas Supreme Court made up mostly of other conservative Republicans.'

"Her own colleagues on the conservative Texas Supreme Court have repeatedly accused her of the same thing. They clearly state that Justice Owen puts her own views above the law, even when the law is crystal clear. Justice Owen's former colleague on the Texas Supreme Court, our new Attorney General

Alberto Gonzales, has said she was guilty of 'an unconscionable act of judicial activism.'

"In another case, Justice Gonzales joined a majority opinion that criticized Justice Owen for 'disregarding the procedural limitations in the statute,' and 'taking a position even more extreme' than was argued by the defendant in the case.

"For the very important D.C. Circuit, the President has nominated another extreme right-wing candidate. Janice Rogers Brown's record on the California Supreme Court makes clear that—like Priscilla Owen—she's a judicial activist who will roll back basic rights. When she joined the California Supreme Court, the California State Bar Judicial Nominees Evaluation Commission had rated her 'not qualified,' and 'insensitive to established legal precedent' when she served on the state court of appeals.

"All Americans, wherever they live, should be concerned about such a nomination to this vital court, which interprets federal laws that protect our civil liberties, workers' safety, and our ability to breathe clean air and drink clean water in their communities. Only the D.C. Circuit can review the national air quality standards under the Clean Air Act and national drinking water standards under the Safe Drinking Water Act.

"This court also hears the lion's share of cases involving rights of employees under the Occupational Safety and Health Act and the National Labor Relations Act. Yet Janice Rogers Brown's record shows a deep hostility to civil rights, to workers' rights, to consumer protection, and to a wide variety of governmental actions in many other areas—the very issues that predominate in the D.C. Circuit.

"Perhaps most disturbing is the contempt she has repeatedly expressed for the very idea of democratic self-government. She has stated that, 'where government moves in, community retreats [and] civil society disintegrates.' She has said that government leads to 'families under siege, war in the streets.' In her view, when 'government advances . . . freedom is imperiled [and] civilization itself jeopardized.'

"Janice Rogers Brown has also written opinions that would undermine civil rights. She has held, for example, that the First Amendment prevents courts from granting injunctions against racial slurs in the workplace, even when those slurs are so pervasive that they create a hostile work environment in violation of federal job discrimination laws.

"President Bush has selected William Myers for the important Ninth Circuit court of appeals. Mr. Myers is a long-time mining and cattle industry lobbyist. He has compared federal laws protecting the environ ment to 'the tyrannical actions of King George' over the American colonies. He has denounced our environmental laws as 'regulatory excesses.' In the Interior Department, he served his corporate clients instead of the public interest. As Solicitor of Interior, he tried to give public land worth millions of dollars to corporate interests. He issued an opinion clearing the way for mining on land sacred to Native Americans, without consulting the tribes affected by his decision—although he took the time to meet personally with the mining company that stood to profit from his opinion.

"William Myers is a particularly inappropriate choice for the Ninth Circuit, which contains many of America's most precious natural resources and national parks, including the Grand Canyon and Yosemite National Park, and which is home to many Native American tribes. . . ."

Senate speech

May 11, 2005

Teddy was a particularly harsh critic of the conduct of the Iraq War as it was managed by Secretary of Defense Donald Rumsfeld. He criticized Rumsfeld directly:

"This war has been consistently and grossly mismanaged. And we are now in a seemingly intractable quagmire. Our troops are dying. And there really is no end in sight. And the American people, I believe, deserve leadership worthy of the sacrifices that our fighting forces have made, and they deserve the real facts. And I regret to say that I don't believe that you have provided either.

"Isn't it time for you to resign?"

Senate Armed Services Committee hearing

June 23, 2005

Rumsfeld replied that he had offered to resign, twice, but President Bush had not accepted his resignation.

Senator Kennedy remained a gadfly to the Bush administration and pointed his finger directly at the administration following the disaster of Hurricane Katrina:

"Americans continue to be moved by the devastation of Hurricane Katrina and its toll on our fellow Americans from New Orleans and in the Gulf Coast region—particularly in Louisiana, Mississippi, Alabama. The human tragedy has brought out the generosity of the American spirit as people have opened their homes and pocketbooks to families uprooted by the storm.

"This is a disaster of biblical proportions. The dimensions of this tragedy almost are beyond human comprehension. And the failures by our government to prepare and to respond run deep and wide.

"Yesterday, the President and the White House spokesman proclaimed that the Administration would not play the blame game. Well Mr. President, this is not a game. This is not some school yard spat. It is about life and death. And most important, it's about getting it right the next time.

"We must be about the work of providing continuing relief to our citizens and rebuilding our communities. But we also cannot delay the important task of determining what went so gravely wrong, and holding accountable those responsible for the tragic failures that Americans have seen so clearly on their televisions and read in their newspapers. . . ."

Senate speech

September 7, 2005

Bearing the Standard

As an influential Democrat for nearly half a century, Ted Kennedy was a fixture at the party conventions

and was known for his booming voice and powerful ora-
tory.

After a hard-fought campaign in 1980 against the incum-
bent president, Jimmy Carter, Ted Kennedy was forced to
concede the party's nomination to his rival. Even though he
had lost the campaign, his keynote address at the Democratic
National Convention in New York City, August 24, 1980, is
widely regarded as the finest of his career:

"My fellow Democrats and my fellow Americans, I have come here tonight not to argue as a candidate but to affirm a cause. I'm asking you—I am asking you to renew the commitment of the Democratic Party to economic justice. I am asking you to renew our commitment to a fair and lasting prosperity that can put America back to work.

"This is the cause that brought me into the campaign and that sustained me for nine months across 100,000 miles in 40 different states. We had our losses, but the pain of our defeats is far, far less than the pain of the people that I have met. . . .

"Our cause has been, since the days of Thomas Jefferson, the cause of the common man and the common woman. . . .

"It is the glory and the greatness of our tradition to speak for those who have no voice, to remember those who are forgotten, to respond to the frustrations and fulfill the aspirations of all Americans seeking a better life in a better land.

"The demand of our people in 1980 is not for smaller government or bigger government but for better government. . . . The task of leadership in 1980 is not to parade scapegoats or to seek refuge in reaction, but to match our power to the possibilities of progress. . . .

"We are the party of the New Freedom, the New Deal and the New Frontier. We have always been the party of hope. So this year let us offer new hope, new hope to an America uncertain about the present, but unsurpassed in its potential for the future.

"For me, a few hours ago, this campaign came to an end. For all those whose cares have been our concern, the work goes on, the cause endures, the hope still lives, and the dream shall never die."

———◦◉◦———

Though he never ran for president after 1980, Teddy Kennedy's endorsement was highly prized by every candidate of his party. He made a dramatic choice early in 2008:

"Every time I've been asked, over the past year, who I would support in the Democratic primary, my answer has always been the same: I'll support the candidate who inspires me, inspires all of us, who can lift our vision.

"It is time again for a new generation of leadership. It is time for Barack Obama."

American University

January 8, 2008

•

"We have looked in the eyes of the young, a young generation that said they're interested in being involved. There is one person, one candidate, one individual who has the ability to bring together that enthusiasm. . . . His name is Barack Obama."

National Hispanic Cultural Center

Albuquerque, New Mexico

January 31, 2008

In May, 2008, doctors announced that Teddy had a malignant brain tumor. Despite the frightening diagnosis, he continued an active campaign schedule and made a dramatic appearance at the party's convention in August:

"I have come here tonight to stand with you to change America, to restore its future, to rise to our best ideals, and to elect Barack Obama President of the United States. . . .

"We are told that Barack Obama believes too much in an America of high principle and bold endeavor, but when John Kennedy called of going to the moon, he didn't say 'it's too far to get there; we shouldn't even try.' Our people answered his call and rose to the challenge, and today an American flag still marks the surface of the moon. . . .

"There is a new wave of change all around us, and if we set our compass true, we will reach our destination—not merely victory for our party, but renewal for our nation.

"And this November the torch will be passed again to a new generation of Americans, so with Barack Obama and for you and for me, our country will be committed to his cause. The work begins anew. The hope rises again. And the dream lives on."

Speech at the Democratic National Convention

Denver, Colorado

August 26, 2008

Wit

"I plan to go into another contact sport, politics."

To Lisle Blackburn, Green Bay Packers coach

1955

When an awkward Congressman James Hanley was unable to give Ted an endorsement, Kennedy quipped, in front of reporters,

"You can tell these guys, Jim. They won't tell anybody!"

Syracuse, New York

January 1980

•

"It is less than a year since the Vienna summit when President Carter kissed President Brezhnev on the cheek. We cannot afford a foreign policy based on the pangs of unrequited love."

Campaign speech at Georgetown University

January 28, 1980

•

"Well, things worked out a little different from the way I thought, but let me tell you, I still love New York."

Speech at the Democratic National Convention
New York City, New York
August 24, 1980

•

"This is, of course, a nonpolitical speech which is probably best under the circumstances. Since I am not a candidate for President, it would certainly be inappropriate to ask for your support in this election and probably inaccurate to thank you for it in the last one."

Speech at Liberty Baptist University
October 3, 1983

•

"You voted for my brother! You voted for my *other* brother! You didn't vote for me! But if you vote for John Kerry, I'll forgive you."

Campaigning for John Kerry,

his fellow Massachusetts senator, for president

Davenport, Iowa

January 2004

Even brain surgery couldn't hold Ted Kennedy down. On emerging from the operating room, he told Vicki,

"I feel like a million bucks. I think I'll do that again tomorrow."

Ted's father-in-law, Edmund Reggie, was an old friend of the senator's. Just six years older than his daughter's husband,

Reggie suggested in 2007 that Kennedy might want to slow down a bit. He said that he thought Ted Kennedy and Daniel Webster would go down as the two greatest senators in American history. Ted's reply:

"What did Webster do?"

About Ted Kennedy

"He came to the Senate as a very young man. In a sense his formative years were in the Senate, as was his maturity. If anyone can be said to be shaped by the institution, it's Ted Kennedy. There are people who are there a long time, who crack the code. That's what he did. He found the Rosetta Stone of how to prosper there."

Ross K. Baker, political scientist

———◆———

Teddy's aide Frank Mankiewicz found the senator at Bobby's hospital bed as Bobby lay dying in Los Angeles and declared:

"I have never, ever, nor do I expect ever, to see a face more in grief."

•

"Uncle Ted was left to pick up the pieces and be harshly judged for his humanity. It all fell on him. If he hadn't stepped up and carried us on his back for the next thirty-plus years, the family would have disintegrated many times before."

Christopher Kennedy Lawton, Ted's nephew

•

"He's the best strategist in the Senate."

Senator Joseph R. Biden Jr.

1986

•

"It is no secret that Ted and I are close friends, even though I am a conservative, he is a liberal; I am a westerner, he is an easterner; I am a physical fitness fanatic, he is — well, never mind."

Senator Orrin Hatch

On the occasion of Ted's 70th birthday

•

"I've described Ted Kennedy as the last lion of the Senate. . . . He remains the single most effective member of the Senate if you want to get results."

Senator John McCain

May 2008

———⚬———

Among the victims of the terrorist attacks on September 11,
2001, were nearly two hundred citizens of Massachusetts.
The senior senator of that great state made it a personal cause
to reach out to the families of every one of those victims.

"I had not heard from one local politician, one medium
politician, or certainly any federal guy. Nothing. He was
the first one to call and offer assistance, or even sym-
pathy, which meant a great deal to all of us."

Sally White, whose daughter, Susan Blair,

had been killed in the attacks

•

"Starting with a 1965 bill that did away with country-
by-country quotas for immigrants . . . Kennedy, 74,
has amassed a titanic record of legislation affecting

the lives of virtually every man, woman and child in the country. With a succession of Republicans, he helped create COBRA, the Americans with Disabilities Act, portable health care, the Family and Medical Leave Act and more than 15 key education programs, including the landmark 1965 Elementary and Secondary Education Act. He also pushed through the deregulation of the airline and trucking industries and the reduction of the voting age to 18. By the late '90s, the liberal icon had become such a prodigious cross-aisle dealer that Republican leaders began pressuring party colleagues not to sponsor bills with him.

"America's Ten Best Senators," *Time*

April 14, 2006

While campaigning for president in Oregon, Senator Barack Obama reacted to news of Kennedy's diagnosis of brain cancer:

"Ted Kennedy is a giant in American political history—he has done more for the health care of others than just about anybody in history, and so we are going to be rooting for him and I insist on being optimistic on how it's going to turn out.

"I think you can argue that I would not be sitting here as a presidential candidate had it not been for some of the battles that Ted Kennedy has fought. He is somebody who battled for voting rights and civil rights when I was a child. I stand on his shoulders."

May 17, 2008